JANE'S 1983-84
MILITARY REVIEW

edited by Ian V. Hogg

Third year of issue

JANE'S 1983-84
MILITARY REVIEW

edited by Ian V. Hogg

Third year of issue

JANE'S

Copyright © Jane's Publishing Company Limited 1983

First published in 1983 by
Jane's Publishing Company Limited
238 City Road, London EC1V 2PU

Distributed in the Philippines and
the USA and its dependencies by
Jane's Publishing Inc,
135 West 50th Street,
New York, NY 10020

ISBN 0 7106 0283 9

Typesetting by D. P. Media Ltd
Hitchin, Hertfordshire

Printed in Great Britain by
Biddles Limited, Guildford, Surrey

Publisher's note
The first compilation in this series, published in October 1981,
was issued under the title *Jane's Military Annual 1981–82*.

Contents

The Military Scene
Ian V. Hogg
9

The ACE Mobile Force
Charles Messenger
21

The Canadian Combat Training Centre
LtCol J. A. English
34

Coast Defence in the 1980s
Edwin Ralph
52

The Underground World of the Land Mine
Terry J. Gander
59

Electronic Warfare
Don Parry
70

The Military Pistol Today
Gilmour Hill
81

New Equipment
92

Low-Intensity Conflict and US Special Operation Forces: Challenge and Response
David C. Isby
100

Military Helicopters
Michael J. Gething
109

Something New from Africa
Ian V. Hogg
128

Light AA Defence for Field Armies
Charles Castle
141

Remotely Piloted Vehicles
Don Parry
156

One Hundred Years Ago
Ian V. Hogg
167

Foreword

In presenting this, our third annual *Jane's Military Review*, we have once more cast our net widely in order to explore some of the less publicized aspects of the military and defence community as well as some subjects which although reasonably well known could do with some extra airing. Therefore it is perhaps a good time and place to try and explain the object behind the *Review*. Our Jane's Yearbooks, as is well-known, exist to provide *facts* – weights, dimensions, ranges, parameters of performance – leaving the reader to make of them what he will. The *Review*, on the other hand, seeks to provide a forum for discussion. Granted that the Ruritanian Army has adopted the XYZ rifle – fact – is that, indeed, the wisest choice they could have made? Are the armies of the world currently addressing the question of anti-aircraft defence in the best way? Is there a future for coast defence? Is the current fashion in pistols entirely correct? Are the Americans going about their Rapid Deployment Force in the right way?

Is the current view of electronic warfare the right one?

These are some of the questions our contributors have elected to discuss in this issue; whether they offer the right answers is not of great importance. What is important is that they at least put forward alternative arguments to the accepted party line and, in this way, might provoke discussion which could lead to at least a reassessment of various problems. For all we know the solutions preferred by the world's armies may be the correct ones, but a little gentle prodding here and there will at least ensure that these solutions are not taken for granted nor given the strength of Holy Writ.

As before we have endeavoured to make the mixture as varied as possible in order to provide something for all tastes and also give readers something fresh to consider. And, as before, we solicit the comments and opinions of readers on the result.

I.V.H.

The Military Scene

Ian V. Hogg

In any consideration of the military events of 1982/83 the Falklands Campaign obviously claims attention, and it was originally our intention to devote some pages to a review of the South Atlantic War. After thinking about it, however, we have decided against it. There are two ways of reviewing such a campaign; the first is the "instant journalism" technique based upon press releases, on the statements of participants, and on the memoirs of others in attendance; the second is a detailed and reasoned analysis carried out when passions have died down and partisanship has cooled off. As to the first, any bookshop will provide the reader with more than sufficient to satisfy him; for the second we feel that sufficient time has not yet elapsed. In our preliminary talks with various members of the forces who served in the Falklands, when the idea of an article was still being contemplated, it became obvious that passions had not died down, nor was partisanship

much cooler than it had been at the height of the battles. Memories of the affair are too recent to tolerate impertinent questions about why courses of action were taken, who did what and why or who failed to do what and why, and any attempt at criticism is likely to be neutralised by references to the casualty roll and the feelings of relatives. We shall, therefore, leave the subject and return to it after a decent interval, by which time more facts will have appeared and feathers will be less easily ruffled.

As we write, the Iran-Iraq conflict is entering its fourth year as "the Forgotten War" so far as the rest of the world is concerned. The most recent communiques from the front indicate that Iran is putting children into battle, to run in front of the advancing infantry in order to detonate mines, an allegation which, if true, suggests a contempt for human life and a spiritual indoctrination which is scarcely credible to the Western mind. It is now obvious that Iraq made its initial attack too soon, before its army was correctly equipped or sufficiently trained, relying upon the dissension within Iran to counterbalance these deficiencies. As we pointed out last year, however, there is nothing like an external

South African troops of the 61 st Mechanized Infantry Battalion exercising near Omuthiya Base, some 140 km (87 miles) south of the Angola-Namibia border. This unit is responsible for a large area of border territory exposed to incursions by SWAPO guerillas and is kept in a high state of training and readiness.

threat to a divided nation to make it sink its differences, or at least relegate them, and discover a new sense of national purpose. This is what happened in Iran, leading to Iraq being smartly rebuffed.

Iraq has since built up its armaments, but has lost the initial impetus; Iran has lost a lot of equipment but has managed, by religious fervour, to motivate its army better than has Iraq, so that the two are again balanced. As a result the war tends to oscillate back and forth without any significant achievements on either side and looks like continuing this way for a long time to come.

Perhaps more attention might have been paid to the Iran-Iraq struggle, and perhaps more support for the protagonists might have appeared from other nations, had not the Lebanon affair occupied so much of the world's attention. "Operation Peace in Galilee" set out to be a limited-objective operation to clear PLO guerillas out of a strip of Southern Lebanon so that Israeli residents south of the border could live without constant harassment by border raids and bombardment. When it became apparent that the PLO were not going to quietly vacate this area but were willing to dispute the matter, the Israelis decided to clear the entire country, shepherding the PLO into the Beirut area. From there, after much political discussion, the besieged guerrillas were permitted to leave for distant parts where they would, apparently, beat their AK47s into ploughshares and mind their own business.

As anyone other than a politician could have foreseen, this simply meant that the PLO guerillas departed by a variety of routes in order to reassemble behind the Syrian front in the Bek'aa valley and resume their war against the Israelis. As has been pointed out with increasing regularity in the press, the Israelis had fewer casualties in the course of "Operation Peace in Galilee" than they have since suffered in the aftermath of what was ostensibly a successful operation. At the moment the jigsaw is being re-arranged as the PLO appear to have fallen out among themselves and with their Syrian guardians.

Some years ago Yasser Arafat complained, in Moscow, "Is it not unjust that I should have to defend myself with primitive arms in the face of the most advanced American weapons?", a cry which was intended to persuade the Soviets into re-equipping his forces with major types of equipment. Whether the hint was taken is doubtful; but certainly the Israeli advance into Lebanon uncovered a sufficient variety of weapons to show that the PLO was far from being the raggle-taggle band of guerillas of popular myth. The PLO, in fact, turned out to be a highly organised and extremely well-equipped force of several brigades, with a useful sub-strata of heavy artillery and rocket weapons, the provenance of which is extremely doubtful. All of this, though, was left behind when the evacuation from Beirut took place (though the departing PLO men did not appear to have been disarmed

very effectively) and it can now be assumed that the PLO is back to its basic infantry concept, provided with little more than small arms and portable rocket launchers. Any heavy support will, in their present situation, have to come from Syria, and the present schism will make such support doubtful.

The other "forgotten war" is the conflict on the South African borders with Angola and Mozambique, a struggle which ebbs and flows depending upon the relative fortunes of the SWAPO and other organisations vis-a-vis their host countries. When they have an ascendancy over their political rivals, then they can afford to go looking for trouble across the border; when they are occupied with protecting their home power base, the cross-border incidents die down, to be replaced by a propaganda war. Their principal advantage appears to be a near-inexhaustible supply of weapons from Communist sympathisers, and it is this which the South Africans have had to counter by developing their own arms industry, as related on other pages.

In Afghanistan the Soviets are discovering what the British discovered a century ago, that the "wily

Above: A platoon of the 61 st Mechanized Infantry patrolling through bush close to the Angolan border. The Ratel 90 infantry fighting vehicle acts as close support and is also a potent anti-tank weapon, should such targets appear in the future.

Below: A comparison between (top) the US M72 66 mm LAW and the Soviet RPG-18.

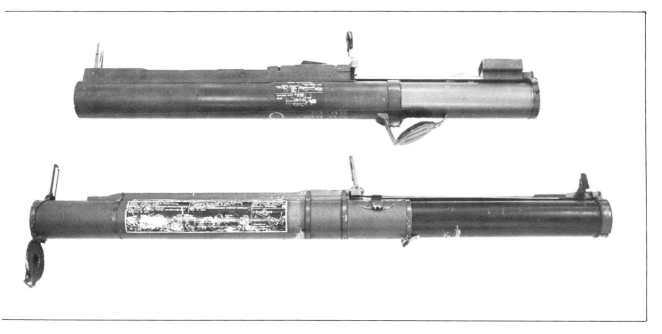

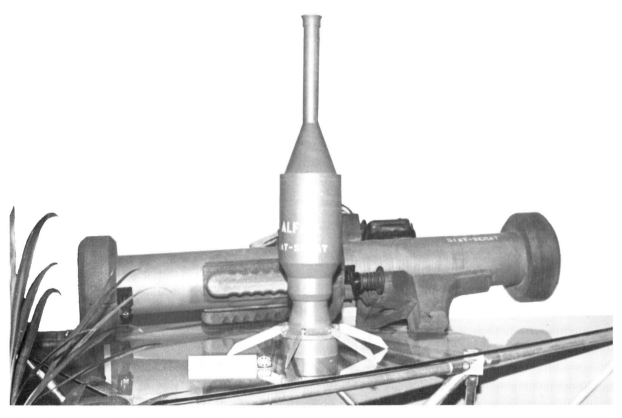

Above: A mock-up of the GIAT-SERAT Alfa anti-tank launcher, the latest countershot design to appear.

Below: The inner workings of the ACL-300 Jupiter, another of the many countershot launchers. The top picture shows the loaded launcher ready for use; below, the propelling charge is fired in the centre of the tube and begins pushing two piston heads outwards; below this, the projectile is being forced out of the muzzle, while the countershot is leaving the rear end; bottom, the projectile is clear and its fins begin to deploy, while the countershot has been ejected and is beginning to disintegrate into individual flakes of plastic. Notice that the two piston heads have been trapped at the ends of the launch tube, so sealing in the 'firing signature' of flash, smoke and noise

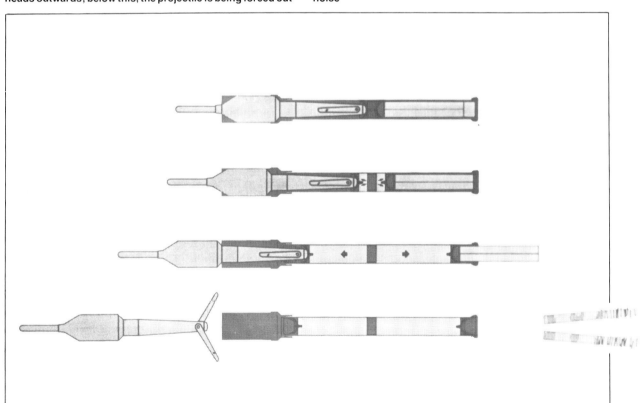

Pathan" is a formidable enemy, one who has forgotten more about guerilla warfare than all the Ho Chih Minhs, Che Guevaras and Mao Tse Tungs put together ever knew. Their initial gambit, to overawe the country with armour, soon proved ineffective, and the Soviets have since turned to an increasing use of helicopter gunships seeing that these give them the mobility and surprise which is their only hope. They have also, and there now seems to be little or no doubt of this, turned to chemical warfare as a means of neutralising whole areas of resistance, allowing them to concentrate their more conventional efforts in other areas.

The morality of chemical warfare has thus appeared once more as a debating point, but it is a question for which we have little time. We have never noticed much morality in warfare, and we would certainly not expect to find it being displayed by the Russians, who know only one way of waging war which is to pull out all the stops and employ any and every weapon which appears to be appropriate. And since their tactics, until now, have shown little success, it is not to be expected that they will refuse to play such a card if it promises results. In this respect the war in Afghanistan, together with the interminable skirmishing in the Indo-China peninsula, recall some aspects of the Spanish Civil War insofar as they appear to be employed as testbeds for weapons, equipment and tactical theories emanating from the Soviet bloc. Warfare, though, differs from scientific laboratory experiments; most of the experimenters in Spain ended by drawing the wrong conclusions from the results they obtained there, and perfecting chemical warfare techniques against defenceless tribesmen is likely to prove useful only if the same sort of warfare has to be repeated in a similar setting at some future time.

On the other hand there are occasions when one finds it very difficult to fathom what the Soviets are trying to do. There have been two examples of this puzzling aspect of Russian behaviour in the past year. Firstly the West obtained specimens of the latest Soviet anti-tank weapon, the RPG-18. After much rumour and surmise this turned out to be no more than a near-carbon copy of the American M72 66 mm shoulder-fired rocket launcher, a device which is now obsolescent and scheduled for replacement throughout NATO. Now, the existing RPG-7 is one of the most advanced and formidable light anti-tank weapons in existence, so the question which immediately springs to mind is "Why should they adopt an obsolescent weapon when they already have an advanced one?"

The second puzzle came with the information that a new pistol had been adopted by the Soviet security services. We had, for some time, known of the existence of a peculiar 5.45 mm cartridge, of Soviet origin, which had led to some lively speculation over the years, but now that it has been positively identified with this pistol the puzzle becomes even greater. It is standard operating procedure for any new Soviet weapon to have a calibre or chambering just sufficiently different from any Western weapon to preclude the use of Western ammunition, and vice-versa, preclude the use of Soviet ammunition in Western weapons. But why should anyone want to develop a bottle-necked pistol cartridge of 5.45 mm calibre for a simple blowback pocket pistol

In spite of the RPG-18, the Warsaw Pact armies are far from backward; this recent photograph shows a Polish soldier with an RPG-7 anti-tank launcher carrying an image-intensifying sight. So far as we are aware, this is a combination as yet untried in the West, where I-I sights are usually applied to either rifles or crew-served weapons.

A misty February morning and the Battleaxe is paraded, probably for the last time. The Battleaxe was acquired in Martinique in 1809 and has been paraded annually on the anniversary of the capture of Fort Desaix ever since, but 74 Battery Royal Artillery, descendants of the original captors, are scheduled for disbandment, the Battleaxe will probably go to the RA Museum in Woolwich, and another minor piece of ceremonial will vanish from the British Army.

to be used by policemen and security troops? Bottle-necked cartridges present problems in blowback weapons; 5.45 mm calibre means a bullet so small that it is only going to be lethal, or even disabling, in the hands of an expert shot at close range. The design of the pistol is such that it could equally well have been chambered in half-a-dozen more practical, and already existing, calibres. The whole thing is so peculiar that it leads to the suspicion that there is a department of the Soviet Ministry of Defence devoted to dreaming up impractical designs simply to keep us guessing.

So far as the RPG-18 is concerned, the conclusion to which we are increasingly drawn is that the object in view is to issue these widely throughout the Soviet infantry so that they may deal more rapidly and effectively with armoured personnel carriers, leaving the more potent and specialised weapons (and their more highly-trained operators) to deal with the main battle tanks, MICVs and other more resistant types of target. To every weapon there is a counter-weapon; and if armies are turning increasingly to the APC for moving their infantry on the battlefield, then obviously the counter is to make every man a potential APC-destroyer. Stop the APCs, put the survivors on their feet, and the battle then comes back to the well-understood and time-honoured combat between opposing foot troops.

Which leads us, by a loose sort of association of ideas, to the thought that for the first time in many years we are seeing a tactical advance which is a technical step backward. Instead of seeing some new and advanced technology being deployed, we suddenly see a cheap and relatively old-fashioned weapon being brought into use. Can this be the first flowering of a move towards simplifying weaponry? For several years there have been people urging "the best is the enemy of the good", "small is beautiful", "simplicate and add lightness" and similar stirring slogans, while on the opposite side of the arena have been the technologists unveiling ever more complex and expensive devices. It has been apparent for some time that no Western nation could possibly hope to equip its troops with the latest technology in any worthwhile quantity, simply because the expense was too great. Many and ingenious have been the excuses offered; qualitative superiority over quantitative has probably been the most convincing. But aviation specialists have recently been facing up to the fact that simple and less expensive fighters appear to have a higher survivability factor in combat than do the high-technology wonders, even though they may not have quite such an impressive weapon load or fire control or whatever. Is there something to be learned here by ground forces?

Not that it is necessary to sacrifice technology in vital areas in order to achieve economies overall. A prime example of this argument is the adoption of wheeled self-propelled guns by the Czechoslovakian Army and now, though so far only in prototype form, by the South African Defence Force. We explored the basic advantages of wheeled SP guns in these pages two years ago, so there is no need to labour the tactical features. But the South Africans have made public some interesting figures which serve to reinforce the arguments we put forward then. Their G6 155 mm wheeled SP is, we are told, some 50 per cent cheaper to build than a comparable tracked vehicle; it uses some 60 per cent less fuel; it requires half the horsepower per ton to move it; it has three times the operating life and twice or three times the interval between overhauls; and it can travel at 90 km/hr (56 mph) on roads and 45 km/hr (28 mph) across country. And for all this, the basic function – firing a shell to 37.5 km (23 miles) range – is unimpaired; it can provide artillery support every bit as effectively as a tracked equipment. In other words in the vital area – the tactical employment of the weapon – technology has been allowed full rein, whilst in the

Another farewell look at a familiar scene; the barrel-straightening shop at the Heckler & Koch factory in Oberndorf. Barrel straightening, a vital part of weapon manufacture, has been performed in this manner for centuries, but has now been replaced by electronically-controlled automatic machinery. (I. V. Hogg)

ancillaries – the method of moving the thing around – simplicity has been the rule.

Some time ago we were in conversation with a military Project Manager who made some cogent remarks on the subject of modern equipment. We had suggested that certain defence fields might be better served if they were given a wider spread of weapons, but his answer made us think again. His argument was simply that it makes better sense to expand the distribution of a tried and tested weapon, even though it might no longer be at the forward edge of technology, than to augment a scanty provision by issuing a new and different weapon of more modern aspect. His point was that the existing weapon already has its spares and stores backup and all its logistic support in being; thus, expanding its distribution to the troops would simply mean making more weapons, but it would not entail the setting up of a completely new supply and logistic system. This is a hard argument to refute, and the only observation we could make was that the theory would only apply to weapons still having a considerable superiority over their target; it would, for example, be pointless to proliferate an anti-tank weapon no longer capable of coping with the putative enemy's main battle tank. The British Army learned that particular lesson the hard way in 1940 when it perpetuated the 2-pounder (40 mm) anti-tank gun in service as the "tried and tested" weapon, at the expense of the 6-pounder

(57 mm), and promptly fell behind in the tank/anti-tank battle. Furthermore, there must always be a point at which the decision has to be taken to abandon the old and press on with the new, and when several million pounds-worth of spares and stock have to be considered, it can only make the decision harder. If we may be forgiven for another historical analogy, we would point to the group of German officers who, in 1938 and after much analysis, determined that a short-case 7 mm cartridge, and an automatic rifle to suit, was the infantry arm of the future. The theory was impeccable, and, indeed, in due course it later gave birth to the assault rifle, but in 1938 the German War Department held stock of about 70 milliard rounds of standard 7.92 mm ammunition, and nobody was willing to be the man who sentenced that lot for scrap. Economics and tactics make hard bedfellows.

Mention of anti-tank weapons brings us to consider the current profusion of such devices either in service or on offer from a variety of manufacturers around the world. Not so long ago anyone with a yearning to design military equipment would appear with a new sub-

Right: The French AMX 40 Main Battle Tank seen for the first time at the Satory IX French Army Exhibition. Based on the existing AMX 30 design it features a new and powerful 120 mm gun, longer chassis and the latest fire control equipment. (A. T. Hogg)

Below: The MIRA (Milan Infra-Red Attachment) night vision device has now entered service with the British Army in Germany and will also equip the French and Federal German forces. It permits the detection of tanks at ranges up to 3 km and their engagement at 1.5 km range. (Aérospatiale)

machine gun, but this passion now appears to be spent (except, it would seem, in the USA) and the shoulder-fired anti-tank launcher is now the fashionable product. There is, of course, an immense economic incentive; given that the scale of distribution in a major army is going to be in the order of two or three disposable launchers per infantry platoon, then a successful design is obviously going to be a money-spinner, but the competition is fierce.

The spur to all this activity has been the thought of a Soviet T-80 main battle tank, and the widely-advertised American discovery of two or three years back, that their existing weapons were incapable of defeating a T-72 head-on. An obvious retort (too obvious, perhaps) was to the effect that if armed with such a weapon it was patently unwise to attack such a target head-on, and much more sensible to stalk around it until it became possible to fire at the engine compartment or some less well protected area of the vehicle. To which the practical infantryman responded by pointing out that the SOP did not permit private stalks, and the integrated defence plan meant that the anti-tank launchers were emplaced with specific arcs of fire, and thus,

given their immobility, they had no choice but to wait for the tank to appear, and in such a case the odds were high that it would be a head-on target when it finally arrived.

The answer in almost every case has been to upgrade the hollow charge warhead in order to defeat more armour, either by improved internal design or by adopting an over-calibre warhead. But the most recent appearances in this field, none of which have yet received formal military approval, seem to be more concerned with the question of the "firing signature", the report and the cfflux of flame and blast which accompanies the discharge of this type of launcher, advertising the firer's position and also rendering it hazardous to use such weapons in a confined space.

The reduction of this signature has been achieved, almost universally, by reverting to the age-old Davis countershot principle. Commander Davis was an American who devised a recoilless gun during the First World War. It was, in strict fact, two guns back to back with a common chamber, and the round of ammunition was a cartridge case with a projectile in each end. The "active" projectile, that which was to be discharged

Another new British equipment, the Centronic SAWES (Small Arms Weapon Effects Simulator) which uses an eye-safe laser on the weapon and a set of detectors on the soldier's body. It allows realistic tactical training by shooting a laser beam at his opponent, the detectors are energized and an alarm sounds, indicating to the wearer that he has been "shot". (Centronic Ltd)

against the enemy, was a conventional shell; the other, known as the countershot, was a package of grease and lead shot. Both were the same weight, and firing the centrally-located cartridge sent them down their respective barrels at the same velocity, the service projectile to go to the target and the countershot to disintegrate, due to air resistance and centrifugal force, a short distance behind the gun. The result of the two countervailing forces was, of course, to render the weapon recoilless.

In later years the countershot was transmuted into a blast of gas through a venturi, this gas being derived from a major portion of the propelling charge – about four-fifths of it. But now the wheel has made a complete revolution and we are back with the countershot, now made from a package of plastic flakes which, en masse, have the necessary balancing characteristic, but which when ejected become individual lightweight particles with poor carrying power which soon flutter to the ground and do little or no damage should they hit anything after ejection. This, though, does very little for the signature unless some method of restraining the

blast of gas can be found, and this has been done by locating the propulsive charge between two piston heads inside the launcher. The projectile sits in front of the forward piston and the countershot behind the rear one. On firing, the pistons are propelled rapidly down the launch tube, pushing the projectile and countershot in their respective directions, but as the pistons reach the ends of the tube so they are trapped and locked into the tube preventing the explosion gas and flame from reaching the open air. This muffles the explosion and reduces the signature to whatever minor disturbance is made by the ejected plastic flakes.

This system first saw use with the MBB 'Armbrust' projector, but it has since appeared on one or two other designs, doubtless with minor differences to avoid patent difficulties. The latest proposal, from the French GIAT-SERAT combine, is to place the propulsive charge inside a folded flexible bag – presumably plastic – between projectile and countershot. On firing the bag is violently expanded along the launch tube, ejecting the two shot elements, but retaining the products of the explosion and muffling the noise of firing. We understand that feasibility firings have proved that the basic idea works, and that now the engineers are busy turning it into a workable weapon. Those of a suitably irreverent turn of mind might care to contemplate some warlike use to which the bag full of gas might be put.

Meanwhile the search goes on for the third generation of anti-tank guided missiles, the "fire-and-forget" or "launch-and-leave" generation. Whilst the present second generation missiles are undoubtedly efficient, their principal defect is that the operator needs to keep his sight aligned with the target during the missile's flight – which may be up to 15 seconds or more – and, in consequence, cannot devote his attention to anything else. This has led to some despondent observations from those concerned with anti-tank defence in Western Europe; in theory the engagement range is 2000 m (2190 yds), but in practice the terrain is such that the soldier is unlikely to be able to fix on a target at much over 1000 m (1090 yds). A main battle tank travelling at full speed can cover about 150 m (165 yds) in the time of a single engagement; allowing for ten seconds to reload and find a fresh target, this means that the missile crew will have time to engage four tanks before the attack arrives at a point below the minimum engagement range of the missile. If there are five or more tanks in the attacking force. . . .

Consequently the fire-and-forget weapon becomes an attractive proposition; as fast as they can be loaded, directed and fired, that fast can the launcher be turned on to another target, leaving the missiles to carry on with their designated target in their own time. Another attraction is that such missiles would become viable in an armoured carrier; at present an APC or MICV armed with a wire-guided missile needs to come to a stop and devote its whole attention to guidance, and while it is so engaged it is, in our view, failing in its primary task which is that of putting the infantry where they need to be. But with a third generation missile, the vehicle commander can "shoot from the hip" at a worthwhile target and carry on with his mission.

There have been various proposals put forward, and several companies are working on projects, though very little hard fact has appeared. The principal problem seems to us to be that of ensuring that the missile sees the right target and then homes on to it; an isolated tank in the middle of a desert would doubtless be a fairly easy proposition, but one particular tank among a couple of dozen, all weaving around the battlefield, with smoke, dust, gunfire and natural terrain features all adding to the confusion, must be a very different matter indeed. The layman might suppose that firing a missile into the thick of the enemy, with the assurance that it would, in any event, home on one of them, would be satisfactory, but most NATO forces teach their anti-tank missile men to be selective: to take out the command tanks, the communication tanks, the specialist vehicles, rather than simply shoot up any tank, and therefore the F&F missile must have this same degree of selectivity. Once aimed at a specific tank, that is the one it has to hit.

After some thirty years of service the British 120 mm BAT recoilless anti-tank gun has been declared obsolete, replaced by the Milan missile. (Ministry of Defence)

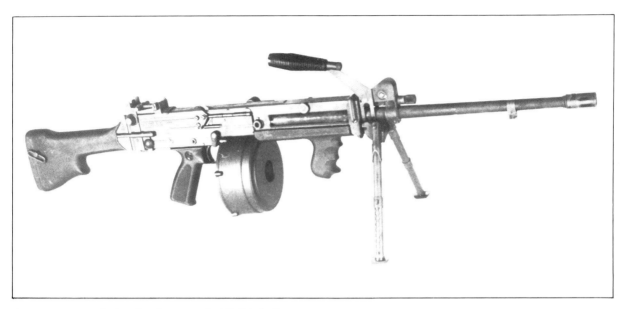

Armaments manufacture is where you find it; this is the Ultimax 5.56 mm light machine gun, developed and manufactured in Singapore. (Chartered Industries of Singapore)

Laser illumination and homing sounds an attractive system, but once again it demands the undivided attention of somebody over a period of time, and, moreover, there seem to be second thoughts about the viability of laser systems in some applications. We spoke encouragingly of Copperhead last year, but even before the words were in print the US Army was retreating from its former stance and cutting back its procurement of Copperhead on the score of poor accuracy and inflated costs. Millimetric wave radar has its attractions, among them the fact that such radar can be a totally passive system, a technique known as "radiometry". This takes advantage of the fact that at very high frequencies, millimetric radar is close to the far infra-red spectrum and the emissions show a tendency to take on near-optical characteristics, notably the appearance of a phenomenon known as "noise temperature", a form of reflectance radiation capable of defining an object by its contrast with its surroundings and capable of being detected by radar-type sensors. This system is being investigated by contractors working on the US Army's Wasp anti-tank missile and also for the STAFF (Smart, Target-Activated, Fire & Forget) 155 mm shoulder-fired anti-armour projectile. But the word we hear around the laboratories is that there is probably four years work ahead before this type of guidance becomes a practical proposition.

Taking one consideration with another then, the twelve months since our last publication does not seem likely to be regarded as a vintage year from the military point of view. South Africa has come out as a producer of armaments; Israel has found a new role as an occupying power rather than as an army given to fast actions and short campaigns; the Soviets are as intransigent as ever over nuclear parity; the designers and scientists are still working on the same projects; and nothing very new has appeared at any military exhibition. Let us be thankful for small mercies; at least no major conflagration has broken out, the SALT talks look like limping along, the Pakistan government is trying to impose some order on the myriad Afghan refugee and resistance parties in order to try and promote a dialogue with the Soviets towards the removal of their toops from Afghanistan, and there are reports that the Americans might have persuaded the Angolan government to get rid of their Cuban guests. Perhaps the next year will surprise us all.

The ACE Mobile Force

Charles Messenger

International cooperation as a British transportation NCO checks off Canadian and Belgian troops about to board an aircraft in North Norway. (HQ UK Land Forces)

The origins of the Allied Command Europe (ACE) Mobile Force lie with General Lauris Norstad, who was Supreme Allied Commander Europe (SACEUR) 1956–62, and the change in NATO's overall doctrine from massive retaliation to flexible response. The growth of Soviet nuclear weapon power and her development of forces, amphibious and airborne, capable of operating anywhere in the world, meant that under the former doctrine the Warsaw Pact had only to put a foot inside NATO territory to unleash a nuclear war in which both sides were likely to suffer severely. Clearly this was an unacceptable state of affairs, and NATO planners began to consider how they could take steps to deter the Warsaw Pact short of an all-out nuclear war.

One aspect which they addressed was the action that NATO should take in the event of a limited Soviet or Warsaw Pact attack aimed merely at seizing territory, either for its strategic value or to use as a bargaining counter. Of particular concern were the two flanks of NATO, northern and southern. These embraced Norway and Denmark on the one hand, and Greece, Turkey and Northern Italy on the other. There were a number of aspects in common to all these areas. First, they had common land frontiers or waterways with Warsaw Pact countries, and indeed are nearer Moscow and the industrial centres of the USSR than other

Above: Volvo over-snow vehicles of the AMF during Exercise "Anorak Express," Northern Norway 1980.

Below: Royal Netherlands Marines on patrol ski past Volvo over-snow vehicles in North Norway.

A Canadian Army Grizzly APC on outpost duty in North Norway during Exercise "Anorak Express". (I. V. Hogg)

NATO countries. Then, in the main there were few NATO forces deployed there, with the bulk concentrated in the Central Region, and each contains NATO Air Defence Ground Environment (NADGE) radar installations. Also, they cover the Soviet Union's sea routes to the west. Thus they were and are vital to the overall NATO defence plan, but also very vulnerable. Yet, if, say, the Russians moved a brigade into Northern Norway, was this justification for launching a nuclear war? Article 5 of the North Atlantic Treaty makes it plain that an attack on one NATO member is an attack on NATO as a whole, and that each member will "assist the Party or Parties so attacked by taking forthwith, individually and in concert with the other Parties, such action as it deems necessary, including the use of armed force, to restore and maintain the security of the North Atlantic area." It was likely, however, that faced with the stark choice of pressing the nuclear button or allowing the Russians to get away with it, the NATO members would merely consult with one another and do nothing more. If the Russians thought the same, the whole concept of deterrence would be in ruins. This much concerned General Norstad.

After some thought, he conceived the idea of a conventional force which could be deployed quickly to either flank in time of threat, and in 1959 announced his intention of setting this up. In early 1960, a working party was formed under General Bruce Clarke to frame the organisation of the force, which would be of brigade

size and multi-national in character. Indeed, it was the latter rather than the strength of the force which was to be its key characteristic, and its object was laid down as "to make clear to any actual or potential aggressor that an attack against one nation would constitute an attack against all members of the Alliance, thereby demonstrating the unity of purpose upon which NATO is based. The presence of soldiers from many nations should cause a potential aggressor to think again. The AMF (ACE Mobile Force) is intended to be an important part of NATO's deterrent." What is particularly significant about the AMF's role as a deterrent is that it was the first indication in concrete form of the move away from massive retaliation, although it would not be until 1967 that flexible response, with the idea of a force structure based on a mix of conventional and nuclear, capable of meeting a wide range of situations, was formally adopted by the Alliance.

By autumn 1960, the working party had completed its studies and AMF was set up. It consists of two elements, land (AMF[L]) and air (AMF[A]). However, the latter has no permanent commander or headquarters. Instead, when activated, it is placed under the operational control of the Allied Tactical Air Force or Regional Air Commander of the area in which AMF[L] is deployed. There are some one hundred aircraft for offensive support operations, fighters and fighter bombers, provided by seven nations. Canada, the Netherlands, Britain and the USA concentrate on the northern flank, while the Belgians, West Germans and Italians take care of the southern flank. As for air transport, each nation is responsible for deploying its own

British ski troops on patrol in Norway. (W. Fowler)

element of AMF[L], but where there are shortfalls, as often happens, the individual countries can call on the US Military Airlift Command (MAC), which also flies in the heavier loads, including heavy lift helicopters.

AMF[L] is made up of the elements of seven member nations – Belgium, Canada, Italy, Luxembourg, Federal Republic of Germany, Britain and the United States. Unlike AMF[A], it does have a small permanent headquarters, which is collocated with that of Central Army Group at Mannheim-Seckenheim in West Germany. The Commander AMF[L] is answerable to SACEUR direct, with AMF[L] being regarded very much as SACEUR's "fire brigade." The Commander himself is rotated among the nations contributing to the Force, and his staff is also multi-national, with, as in the rest of NATO, English being the official language. As for the national contributions, each is based on a battalion group, although the larger nations provide additional elements as well.

The Belgian contribution consists of a battalion of the Parachute Commando Regiment, which is rotated in the role every five months, but remains based in Belgium. In addition, and permanently dedicated to AMF[L], are a battery of 105 mm howitzers and an anti-tank company equipped with the Milan anti-tank

guided weapon (ATGW). The Canadians contribute a battalion from their Special Service Force based in Canada. This is mechanised with a mixture of M113A1s and the wheeled Grizzly, which is built by General Motors of Canada under licence from the Swiss Mowag Company, as well as having specialist over-snow vehicles. There are also a 105 mm pack howitzer battery and a flight of tactical lift helicopters. Italy is represented by a battalion of Alpini, a 105 mm pack howitzer battery and, if required, a field hospital, while Luxembourg contributes the 1st (Light) Infantry Battalion.

The Germans provide 262 Parachute Battalion and a 105 mm pack howitzer battery, and both are airport-able with UH-1D Hueys. They also have a field hospital, with capacity of 100 beds, and a signals company, which gives telephone and teletype communications, as well as a courier service and message centre for the Force. The British, too, have a variety of troops in their contingent. The battalion is currently 1st Bn The Parachute Regiment, which is based on Salisbury Plain, and this is supported by a 105 mm light gun battery. However, they also provide the Force Artillery Headquarters, which is based on a normal regimental HQ. Furthermore, it has a reconnaissance squadron equipped with Scorpion and Scimitar light reconnaissance tanks, which is provided by the Blues and Royals at

Above: German Army helicopter lifting ammunition for a Belgian artillery battery during an AMF exercise in Portugal.

Below: German mountain artillery with their 105 mm howitzer during Exercise "Ardent Ground," Portugal 1981.

Above: Royal Air Force Harriers, part of the AMF air component, on Tromsø airfield, North Norway.

Below: RAF Puma helicopter hooking on to a Belgian 105 mm howitzer to lift it to a new gun position during exercises in Portugal.

Windsor, a radio troop for communications between Force HQ and the individual units, and half the Force helicopter strength in the form of four Pumas from No 38 Group RAF. Finally, but by no means least, there is the logistic support battalion headquarters, but more about this aspect later. The Americans provide 1st Battalion (Airborne) 509th Infantry, which is based at Vicenza in Italy, an M102 105 mm howitzer battalion, engineer company, aviation company which gives Commander AMF[L] his command and control helicopter assets, and an administrative company, again in support of the Force Headquarters.

The most important point to note, apart from the multi-national aspect, is that the Force is very lightly equipped, but quickly deployable. This reflects the concept behind AMF, that of deterrence through NATO solidarity rather than sheer "muscle," although it is prepared to fight if it has to. If this was the case, it would be there to buy time while further NATO forces were deployed to the area. However, it is its ability to deploy rapidly in time of tension which is the key to AMF.

Belgian Para-Commando gunners who form part of the AMF artillery strength.

Above: American airborne artillery firing an M102 105 mm howitzer during an AMF artillery exercise in Portugal. (A. T. Hogg)

Below: Royal Air Force Puma helicopter of 38 Group RAF about to lift a Portuguese 105 mm howitzer during an AMF artillery exercise. (A. T. Hogg)

British and Canadian troops moving rations in the AMF Logistic Base, North Norway.

Should tension develop on one of the NATO flanks, the matter would be first discussed by the North Atlantic Council, the highest NATO decision making body. If it was decided that a show of force was needed to help defuse the situation, the NATO Military Committee would be instructed to produce this and they would, if the threatened member had asked or agreed that forces additional to those already based in its own territory were required, almost certainly call upon SACEUR to deploy the ACE Mobile Force. The order would be passed to AMF[L] HQ, which would alert the national contingents, and SACEUR would also alert member nations providing elements of AMF[A] direct, as well as the Regional Air Command involved. The latter would then deploy as ordered by the Regional Air Command.

The AMF[L] elements would be deployed using their own national lift resources, although, as has been mentioned earlier, they could call on MAC for additional help. Crucial to the deployment phase is the Force Movements Detachment, which comes under the logistic support battalion, and is responsible for coordinating the movement of both troops and equipment to the country under threat, and then moving them out to the deployment area. It is a very versatile unit, and is capable of simultaneously running movement operations at a port, railhead and airfield. As the troops arrived, so would a Base Logistics Support Company (BLSC) be set up, made up from National Support Elements (NSEs) and a host nation support unit. The latter is particularly significant, because, once in-country, AMF[L] is entirely reliant on the host nation for all logistic back-up. Thus, supply runs for the Force are done by host nation vehicles and drivers and bulk stores are drawn from host nation depots. This means that, in view of the different types of equipment and even varying eating habits, the host nation, be it Norway, Denmark, Turkey, Greece or Italy, has to have depots set up accordingly. The BLSC, having set up the Force base area, with its supply and maintenance installations, is then responsible for the processing of all supplies and maintenance to the forward troops. However, it might well be that the Force's deployment area is at some distance from the BLSC, which must of necessity be close to the host country's logistic installations. In this event, a Forward Logistics Support Company (FLSC) is deployed, and this establishes a forward administrative area, using forward detachments of the NSEs. As for the fighting

Maintenance of an RAF Puma helicopter, part of the AMF helicopter force.

element of the Force, although answerable direct to SACEUR, it would in the event of hostilities be placed under the operational control of the local NATO commander. Thus, if deployed to the northern flank, AMF[L] would come under CinC Allied Forces Northern Europe, and in the south, CinC Allied Forces Southern Europe. The two CinCs then might well further delegate operational control to the relevant subordinate commander in whose area the Force was deployed.

Obviously, AMF needs to practise its role, and it does this in a variety of ways. Most important are the major exercises held annually. The aim is to try and hold one on each flank each year, and these always have "Express" in their nicknames, thereby emphasising the requirement of the Force to be able to deploy quickly if it is to be effective in its aim of deterrence. Thus, typical nicknames are "Arctic Express" and "Marmara Express." Apart from the obvious training value of these both for the staffs and the troops, the fact that AMF frequently demonstrates its ability to deploy

quickly is a deterrent in itself, and there is no doubt but that the Warsaw Pact does take a great interest in these exercises. There are also a number of Command Post exercises, aimed at practising staff procedures, and gunnery camps are held for the AMF artillery. At unit level, although each member nation of the Force has a prime responsibility to one flank, each unit must be capable of operating on either. This means being able to fight in the snowbound wastes of Northern Norway, the flat agricultural terrain of Schleswig-Holstein and Denmark, the mountains of North-East Italy and Greece, and the deserts of Turkey. This is no easy task, especially when units are either rotated in the AMF role, as with Britain, or conscripts are involved, as with the majority of the nations involved with the Force. Indeed, this has been the major brake in the past in deploying the complete AMF to either flank, and the only possible solutions are either for individuals to have longer tours with AMF units, which means reliance on volunteers – not easy for conscript armies – or to enlarge the AMF to twice its present size and have two forces, one dedicated to each flank.

There are, of course, other problems with which the Force has to contend, and these are brought about

Above: Supplies coming ashore through an ice-strewn fiord on Norway.

Below: A British infantry support company about to come ashore from a landing craft in a Norwegian fiord. (I. V. Hogg)

The end of the line; a British infantryman on outpost duty in North Norway.

mainly by its multi-national character. Thus, there is a wide range of equipment types used by the Force, which creates problems of interoperability, as well as making life difficult for the logisticians. Yet, this is something which NATO as a whole has had to grapple with for the past thirty years. Nevertheless, it would be a significant move towards greater standardisation within the Alliance if a start was made by laying down that the AMF units should have common equipment. Then, although English is the official language of the Force, there are still linguistic problems, and the only

way in which this can be overcome is by extensive use of liaison officers at all levels. The fact, too, that individual elements have to deploy from some many different locations is not wholly satisfactory, and the ideal would be to permanently collocate them. However, in terms of barracks, and the costs of stationing troops in foreign countries, this would be difficult to achieve.

Nevertheless, in spite of the apparent difficulties, the experience of the past twenty years has made the Force surprisingly efficient, and there is no doubt that its deployment systems do work, being much helped by establishing common procedures among the various units. It also provides an ideal opportunity for the individuals within the Force to mix and operate at close quarters with their allies, and all who have served with the ACE Mobile Force have come away broadened by the experience. But, above all, it remains a vital tool of NATO deterrence. As to the future, it is quite possible that the scope of the Force might be broadened. Recent NATO concern over out-of-area operations, those designed to deal with threats to the Alliance outside its immediate sphere of interest (Middle East oil is a good example) have led to realisation of the need for Rapid Deployment Forces (RDF). As yet, only the Americans are taking concrete steps towards this, and they are concerned that Europe is not demonstrating the same will in grappling with this problem. However, AMF is such a force and it might be possible, using it as a base, to establish a true multi-national NATO RDF, which could deter a potential aggressor to NATO's interests outside Europe as the AMF does on the flanks of NATO at present.

The commander of a Canadian Grizzly APC guarding a vital crossing somewhere north of the Arctic Circle. (I. V. Hogg)

Above: Portuguese troops collecting their lunchtime wine ration during an AMF artillery exercise. (A. T. Hogg)

Below: Armoured ambulance of the Canadian element to the AMF, during an exercise in Norway. (HQ UK Land Forces)

The Canadian Combat Training Centre

LtCol J. A. English, PPCLI

CFB Gagetown, showing its location close to the port of Saint John. (CFB Gagetown)

Canadian Forces Base Gagetown to the west of the St. John River in the Province of New Brunswick is one of the largest land force training areas in the Commonwealth. Taking its name from the small Queens County shire town of Gagetown, originally known as Grimcross but later renamed in honour of General Thomas Gage,[1] commander-in-chief of British forces in America at the time of Bunker Hill, Lexington and Concord, CFB Gagetown sprawls over some 1110 square kilometres (427 sq miles) and represents one-seventieth or 1.4 per cent of the entire territory of New Brunswick. Located about 15 km south of the provincial capital of Frederic-

ton, it is the home of the Canadian army's Combat Training Centre. The latter is the principal training base at which basic and advanced soldierly skills are taught within Mobile Command, the largest functional command in the Canadian Forces, the mission of which is to maintain combat-ready land and tactical air forces to meet Canada's varied defence commitments. Each year close to 3000 officers and men of armoured, artillery and infantry persuasions undergo training at the Combat Training Centre. Here it is not unusual to have 15 courses and other field force units on the ranges at the same time, all conducting live firing practices with the deadliest weapons the Canadian army possesses.

[1] General Gage received a grant of 100 000 acres of land in this area in 1765.

That the Province of New Brunswick was chosen as the home of the Canadian army's most important training base appears most appropriate in light of Canadian historical and political evolution. One of the four original charter provinces of Canada and a British colony since 1784, New Brunswick retains on its provincial coat of arms, granted by Queen Victoria in 1868, the Latin inscription *Spem reduxit*. Literally meaning "Hope restored," this motto can be traced back, along with the story of New Brunswick as a province, to the surrender of the Southern Army of Edward, Lord Cornwallis, at Yorktown, Virginia, in October, 1780. By terms of this capitulation American Loyalists were deemed outlaws and traitors, to be killed, maltreated or exiled as each new American state might choose. Many of them consequently thronged to New York, where began in the late summer of 1793 a mighty mass migration to Nova Scotia, "probably the most dramatic episode in the whole story of Loyalist wanderings in the New World." It was this group that formed the foundation of the Province of New Brunswick, which was created on the partition of Nova Scotia in 1784.

Mainly at the urgings of Sir Guy Carleton,[1] who had successfully defended Quebec against Arnold's Expedition in 1781, Loyalist resettlement lands were obtained in the valley of the St. John River in what was then Sunbury County of Nova Scotia, or "Nova Scarcity" as the embittered Loyalists were sometimes wont to call their new homeland. As Carleton saw it, the settlement of the Royal Provincial Army in regimental blocks would effectively secure these largely untapped Canadian lands for the Crown and provide a barrier to any northward expansion of the rebel colonies. The border, in short, would be held by battle-hardened troops who could be trusted to fight faithfully for King George III, whose portrait, incidentally, still occupies the *place d'honneur* in the New Brunswick provincial legislature. In any case, throughout 1783 the weary and battered regiments, their families and civilian sympathisers – now collectively and endearingly referred to as United Empire Loyalists – poured into St. John. Scores of settlements sprang up throughout southern New Brunswick, colonels and officers taking up land along with their men. The names of the regimental blocks still sound, on reading, like a distant drum roll: King's Orange Rangers, South Carolina Royalists, King's American Dragoons, New Jersey Volunteers, Queen's Rangers, King's Caroline Rangers, Royal Fencible Americans, New York Volunteers, King's American Regiment, Loyal American Regiment, Tarleton's British-American Legion, and the Armed Boatmen of Long Island.

Though the system of settlement on regimental blocks soon broke down under economic pressure, the Province of New Brunswick retained a strong military tradition. British regulars remained stationed in Fredericton as part of the Imperial defence system until 1866, and active militia and volunteer organisations, as well as the services of individual New Brunswickers, have since added to the Province's rich military history. The Carleton and York Regiment, for example, was awarded more battle honours than any other Canadian unit in the Second World War.

The creation of CFB Gagetown, or Camp Gagetown as it was formerly termed, is of relatively more recent origin. When war clouds loomed over both Korea and Europe in the 1950s the establishment ceiling for Canada's three regular services was raised from the 51 000 figure set in 1946 to 100 000, of which the army share was 55 000. In 4 May, 1951, the Minister of National Defence announced the Canadian government's intention to form a brigade group for service with NATO land forces in Europe. It was at the same time decided to reorganise the home army on a divisional basis, which objective in turn identified the need for a large training area with certain characteristics. In the first instance, it was imperative that the new base be near an Eastern Canadian all-weather port. It also had to be suitable for all types of training and be big enough to accommodate the manoeuvres of a 17 000-man division. It was stipulated furthermore that the base be established with as little disturbance as possible to the civil population. An extensive survey subsequently conducted in Nova Scotia and New Brunswick eventually concluded that the area currently occupied by Base Gagetown was the best possible place. In the summer of 1952 the Federal Government accordingly announced that a permanent military base and training area would be built in Queens and Sunbury counties in the vicinity of Gagetown. Clearing and construction commenced in 1953 and the base officially opened in 1955.

Although minimal disturbance of the civil population was attempted, much of the property that eventually formed the greater part of Base Gagetown had to be expropriated. Between 2000–3000 people were uprooted and evicted from their homesteads, much as had been the original Acadien settlers who preceded them decades before. In most cases it was a heart-wrenching process, for many families had lived in the region for up to 150 years. Regrettably, evacuation initially also exerted an adverse effect on the economy of the surrounding area, causing the collapse of some small businesses and reducing certain markets at least temporarily. It was argued, nonetheless, that on the whole the upheaval was less traumatic than it would have been had any other suitable area of the Maritimes been selected. To be sure, businesses and commercial farms were not all that heavily concentrated in the Gagetown area, and, given the amount of compensation paid by the Federal Government, those who had successful businesses were enabled to establish them-

---

[1] Thomas Carleton, brother of Sir Guy, Lord Dorchester, was the first governor of New Brunswick, serving in such capacity until 1817.

Above: Blue Mountain Camp, one of the two field camps established in the southern half of the training area. (CFB Gagetown)

Below: The Gagetown training area is 80 percent forest. (CFB Gagetown)

selves elsewhere. Finally, the ensuing development that devolved on the local region and the large payroll of armed forces personnel eventually brought immeasurable gains to the overall economy of the Province.

All factors considered, Base Gagetown measured up well to the requirements established. Its permanent campsite is roughly 110 km (68 miles) from the port of St. John by rail and about 90 km (56 miles) by road. The approximately 275 000 acres (111 000 hectares) that make up Base Gagetown are bounded by an egg-shaped 120-mile (193 km) perimeter, about 26 miles (50 km) long and 22 miles (35 km) wide at its greatest dimensions. The north end of the base, where the main campsite has been built, its adjacent to the town of Oromocto; the south end is only 25 miles (40 km) from St. John. A public north-south paved highway runs through the middle of the training area for a distance of some 20 miles. The training area contains within itself some 450 miles of unpaved but improved roads. Geographically the largest training area used by the Canadian Army CFB Gagetown is also the most intensively used site in the Defence Department's land inventory.

The Gagetown training area is basically divided by the Otnabog River into northern and southern halves. The northern half contains several numbered training areas and a static range impact area into which can be fired artillery, mortars, tanks, anti-armour weapons, and small arms. This portion also includes tracked and wheeled driving ranges. The southern half, on the other hand, contains a general manoeuvre area and a rugged terrain sector, both of which are further subdivided into numbered areas. Because the southern portion is at least about one and a half hours driving time by tracked vehicle from the main campsite, two field camps have been established in the south: Camp Petersville in the general manoeuvre area and Camp Blue Mountain in the rugged terrain sector. Interestingly, only around 54 000 acres of this vast training area have been cleared of primary growth in support of military training and it remains a constant concern, given the rate of secondary growth, to ensure they remain cleared.

Characterised by a topography that ranges from gently undulating to extremely rugged terrain with steep ridges, the Gagetown training area lends itself to a variety of training. There are in the general manoeuvre area open stretches with scattered woods, ideal for both infantry and tank tactical exercises. Thick woods, and swamps resulting from peculiar watershed properties, simulate in other areas near to jungle conditions. There are also mountains, which, though not very high, do provide some facility for conducting mountain warfare training. The temperate climate of Gagetown is, of course, quite similar to that of Northwest Europe, except for greater snowfall.

The CFB Gagetown main campsite contains upwards of 200 permanent buildings and can provide

Practice at rappelling down a rockface in the Rugged Training Sector. (CFB Gagetown)

accommodation for about 3500 troops. Within the campsite proper there are some 20 miles of paved roads and seven miles of underground tunnels that carry water, heat, electrical, telephone and other services to buildings. The local water purification plant has a capacity of 3 000 000 gallons per day. Camp Argonaut, the Atlantic provinces army cadet camp, is adjacent to the main campsite and provides seasonal accommodation for more than a thousand cadets and staff each year. The town of Oromocto (an Indian word meaning "Deep Water") lies to the west and north of the campsite at the confluence of the St. John and Oromocto Rivers. It includes the 2200 permanent married quarters originally constructed to house the Gagetown regular military establishment, currently holding around 3500. Interestingly, though Oromocto is a civilian

Above: A Canadian Leopard CIA1 tank firing at dusk. (CFB Gagetown)

Below: An M109 155 mm howitzer, one of the equipments of the Artillery School at Gagetown. (CFB Gagetown)

A Leopard tank practising with live ammunition in the manoeuvre area. (CFB Gagetown)

community it had for a period a civic government slightly different from other such communities in New Brunswick. From 1969 to 1971 the town was governed by a mayor and six councillors, one of the councillors being appointed by the Governor-General-in-Council (Federal) and another by the Lieutenant-Governor-in-Council (Provincial). Today the governing body of Oromocto consists of elected members from both the civil and military communities.

The first large-scale exercise was held at Camp Gagetown in the summer of 1954 when the 3rd Canadian Infantry Brigade moved in for six weeks training. The next summer 1st Canadian Infantry Division conducted a complete formation exercise at Gagetown, the first such training ever carried out in Canada. Divisional size concentrations continued to be conducted until 1964, after which brigade concentrations were the norm up to 1970. That year marked a major defence review, prompted by the official unification of the Canadian Forces in February 1968, one result of which was the elimination of the 3rd Canadian Infantry Brigade, stationed at Camp Gagetown, from the order of battle. Significantly, the Minister of National Defence had already announced in September 1969,

that a Combat Training Centre, to include the Combat Arms School recently formed at CFB Borden, was to be established at CFB Gagetown. Between 1970 and 1976 this formation-level organisation was to evolve from a brigade group of the field force with operational responsibilities to the headquarters complex responsible for the coordination and support of all arms training.

A Combat Arms School had, of course, been formed as early as November 1966, when the Royal Canadian Armoured Corps School and the Royal Canadian School of Infantry had been joined together in Camp Borden, Ontario. Essentially consisting of an armoured and an infantry wing initially, CAS (Borden) was this time placed under Canadian Forces Training Command, which, along with other designated "functional" commands,[1] had come into being as a natural consequence of the 1964 integration of naval, army and air force staffs under a single Chief of Defence Staff and the subsequent adoption of the Royal Canadian Air Force's organisational structure. One cannot say, however, that cost effectiveness was the only driving force behind this amalgamation of corps schools. The philosophy of a combined arms school was not a new

---

[1] The other functional commands were: Maritime, Mobile, Air Transport, Air Defence, and Materiel.

Camp Argonaut, the cadet training camp, is adjacent to the main base. The background gives some idea of the type of terrain in which the base has been set up. (CFB Gagetown)

idea. One of the most persistent lessons of the Second World War was the absolutely vital requirement for the cooperation of all arms. Within Commonwealth armies in particular tank-infantry cooperation remained, in the judgement of many officers such as the New Zealander, General Sir Howard Kippenberger, the *primary* tactical problem of the war. He in fact recorded that in the Middle East "there developed at one stage throughout the British Eighth Army . . . a most intense distrust, almost hatred . . . of friendly armour." This was in direct contrast to the German experience in which the principle of the "Cooperation of Arms" came close to being enshrined. This principle was at least understood in the Canadian Army, for when the old single arms schools were being re-established in 1946 many battle experienced instructors and staffs at the time spoke of the need for a type of combined arms school to enhance battle effectiveness.

Interestingly, the Royal Canadian School of Infantry could trace its history back to the formation in 1883 of "practical schools of Military Instruction," in particular "A", "B", and "C" companies of the Infantry School stationed at Fredericton, St. John, and Toronto. In 1885 a Mounted Infantry School was opened in Winnipeg and a fourth Infantry School was established in London, Ontario. The Royal Canadian Armoured Corps School, on the other hand, while perhaps rooted in the 1883 institution of a Cavalry Corps School at Quebec and the formation of a Canadian Tank Corps in 1918, cannot really trace back

beyond 1936. In that year a Tank Training School was established in London, Ontario, using as training vehicles several Carden-Loyd machine-gun carriers. The school was relocated in Camp Borden and renamed "The Canadian Armoured Fighting Vehicles Training Centre" in 1938, during which year it also took delivery of two Vickers Mark VI light tanks – Canada's first. The first commandant of the CAFVTC was Major F. F. Worthington, who returned in April of that same year from courses at the Royal Tank School at Bovington and the Mechanical Engineering Establishment at Farnsborough. The acknowledged founder of the Canadian armoured corps, he saw the delivery of an additional 14 light tanks on the actual eve of the declaration of the Second World War.

In 1946, as a result of a post-war Canadian Army reorganisation, the Royal Canadian Armoured Corps School (which succeeded the CAFVTC) and the Royal Canadian School of Infantry were collocated in Camp Borden "to permit all possible collective training between these two arms." The Royal Canadian School of Artillery had, of course, already been established in Camp Shilo, Manitoba, the previous year. The oldest regular component of the Canadian land forces, the artillery corps had been formed in 1871 on the withdrawal of British forces from Canada. In that year two batteries were established to man the fortifications and armament of Quebec and Kingston. Later designated "A" and "B" Batteries, they served from 1872 as Royal Schools of Gunnery for the training of militia artillery. Over the years additional Royal Schools sprung up in Victoria (coastal and anti-aircraft), Winnipeg, Calgary, Petawawa, Halifax, Camp Hughes, Seaford (England),

Picton (anti-aircraft), and Shilo; the last eventually serving as the Royal Canadian School of Artillery.

At the same time that he announced the establishment of a Combat Training Centre, the Minister of National Defence further directed that the Canadian Forces School of Artillery (as it had been redesignated under Training Command) would be incorporated into the Combat Arms School, which also included the Francophone Training Detachment at CFB Valcartier, Quebec. In May 1970, both CAS (Borden) and the Canadian Forces School of Artillery were reallocated from Training Command to Mobile Command; between May and November of that year they removed to Gagetown to become part of a greater Combat Arms School. Concurrently a portion of the Tactical Air Operations School moved from CFB Rivers, Manitoba, and joined the Combat Arms School. The Francophone Training Detachment remained for the time being at CFB Valcartier. The role given to the CAS at

this juncture was to conduct combat arms training in accordance with approved doctrine and standards.

The CAS training organisation that was initially adopted at the newly created CTC was really quite revolutionary, the not surprising result, perhaps, of a forces-wide unification process that often appeared bent on change purely for change's sake. Originally set up in Borden before the move of CAS to Gagetown, the new organisation was based on divisions and companies structured according to the nature of their "functional" activities. A Command Division, for example, was responsible for all leadership, tactics, tactical air, and special warfare training; a Weapons Division was responsible for all direct and indirect fire training. Execution of training was actually carried out by integrated companies commanded by majors who responded to a highly centralised coordination agency within the headquarters staff. In the main, the old Royal Canadian Infantry Corps Wing was replaced by a "Basic Infantry Division," while other former infantry functions became the responsibility of various integrated companies. Direct Fire Company, for example,

Sniper training is one of the functions of the Infantry School. (CFB Gagetown)

Above: Indoor training has its place; radio operators for all three combat arms receive their basic instruction at Gagetown. (CFB Gagetown)

Below: Individual training is not neglected; here two artillery surveyors practise their art in sub-zero weather. (CFB Gagetown)

Above: Training in water crossing for armoured vehicles, supervised by instructors in an accompanying boat. (CFB Gagetown)

Below: Simulator training for armoured vehicle drivers. (CFB Gagetown)

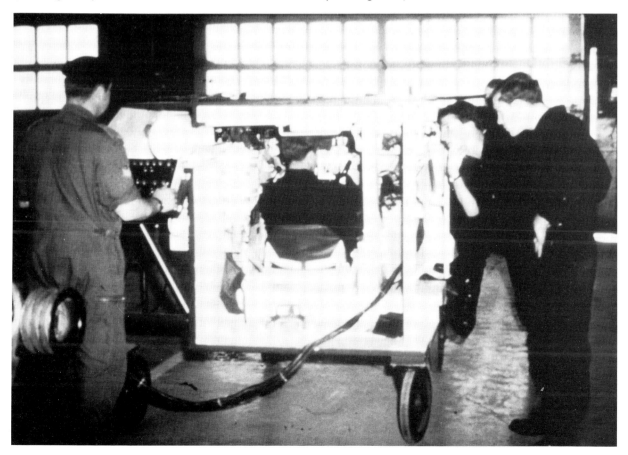

A Carl Gustav 84 mm RCL gun crew in the live firing area.
(CFB Gagetown)

included tank gunnery, infantry small arms, and armoured defence; Leadership Company conducted officer training for all armoured, artillery, and infantry candidates; Indirect Fire Company comprised both field guns and infantry mortars; Tactics Company was a high-powered study organisation concerned mainly with the newly instituted all arms Combat Team Commanders Course; and Environmental Company looked after special warfare training.

Although the foregoing system was made to work, it did give rise to certain complications and vagaries, not the least of which was the difficulty of identifying the traditional arms as entities serving harmoniously with one another. The one combat arm that suffered the greatest identity crisis was, of course, the infantry. Whereas the artillery establishment remained reduced but intact as Indirect Fire Company and the armour as Direct Fire Company, the infantry was principally relegated to recruit training. Advanced infantry training was thought to have suffered accordingly. The headiness of the times had actually been such that the traditional grouping of arms into armour, artillery, and infantry was cursorily dismissed as having little relationship to function.

A number of organisational studies were subsequently conducted, on completion of which a new organisation order was issued in March 1972. In compliance with this order divisions and companies were replaced by departments (Annex A refers). All former infantry functions not within the purview of Basic Infantry Division/Department were now placed under an additional controlling agency, namely, "Infantry Department." At the same time, Indirect Fire Company became Artillery Department and Direct Fire Company, which included driver maintenance and communications/surveillance, became Armour Department. Tactics Department, commanded by a lieutenant-colonel, continued to conduct the Combat Team Commanders Course, land environmental training for pilots, air support officers courses, and ground forward air controllers courses; it also served as the doctrinal focus for all combined arms training. This 1972 reorganisation, which additionally went some way towards integrating CAS and CTC headquarters, was punctuated by the CAS Commandant of the time with the following statement: "When it is necessary for us to change to improve our ability to perform our role, we will change. When it is not necessary to change we will not change."

As training continued, however, it reinforced the view that military function was more properly determined by the requirements of the battlefield than by peacetime organisational theory. A strong movement that advocated the need for three separate corps or branch departments within the CAS accordingly

A 105 mm howitzer battery deployed and camouflaged in the manoeuvre area. (CFB Gagetown)

CAS Organisation Number 3 (1972)

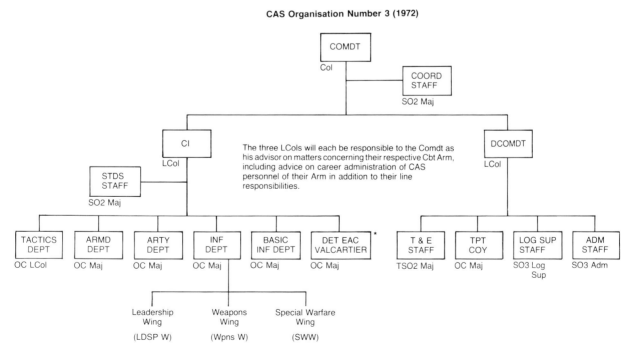

The three LCols will each be responsible to the Comdt as his advisor on matters concerning their respective Cbt Arm, including advice on career administration of CAS personnel of their Arm in addition to their line responsibilities.

* Detachment L'Ecole Des Armes de Combat

Above: The vast manoeuvre area permits the most realistic types of training for drivers of vehicles such as this Cougar APC. (CFB Gagetown)

Below: A general view of the manoeuvre area, showing the scrub terrain. (CFB Gagetown)

developed. In April, 1974, Basic Infantry and Infantry Departments were combined to form one single Infantry Department under a lieutenant-colonel. The officers commanding Armour and Artillery schools were also upgraded at this time to equivalent rank. School support resources and demonstration troops were concurrently centralised under two support groups; respectively, Field Support Group and Training Support Group. Though this structure was considered by many at the time, and even afterwards in retrospect, to be the optimum, it would eventually falter for a lack of resource support.

Principal training emphasis at Gagetown during this period, according to the then CTC Commander, Brigadier-General Radley-Walters, DSO, MC, CD, was that of "the trinity of the infantry, armour, and artillery . . . forming the main pillars in our new Combat Arms School." Describing "an isosceles triangle, with the artillery the supporting base and the infantry and armour the manoeuvrable sides," he went on to place Tactics Department at the apex "designed to establish and influence the common tactical doctrine for all three. . . . the inherent strength of the school

grow(ing) from this philosophy and motivat(ing) the students who are trained there." The need for mutual cooperation between the three arms and the requirement for balanced groupings was constantly stressed. The clear responsibility of the CTC/CAS complex was to impress upon all students the principle of the "Cooperation of Arms" and to have them pass it on, thus "keeping the art alive."

Problems related to field service support, certain resource shortages, and some duplication of effort nonetheless forced further review of the CTC, CAS, and CFB Gagetown organisational structure. Belonging to a "select" group such as the CAS was thought to have a "divisive effect on staff relationships" within the Gagetown military establishment. A major realignment was consequently effected in March 1977, with the result that the Combat Arms School "ceased to exist as an entity, though its essential function remained unchanged." Regarded by some as a "backwards step", this decision had the effect of integrating the

A spectacular night firing demonstration on one of the many small arms ranges. (CFB Gagetown)

OPS and TRG DIV

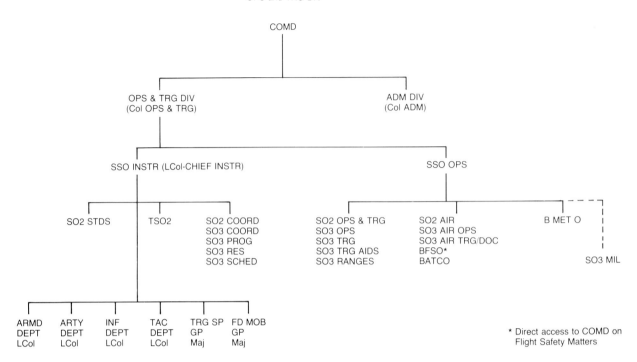

```
                              COMD
                               |
         ┌─────────────────────┴─────────────────────┐
   OPS & TRG DIV                                   ADM DIV
   (Col OPS & TRG)                                 (Col ADM)
         |
   ┌─────┴──────────────────────┐
SSO INSTR (LCol-CHIEF INSTR)                    SSO OPS
```

SSO INSTR (LCol-CHIEF INSTR)			SSO OPS		
SO2 STDS	TSO2	SO2 COORD	SO2 OPS & TRG	SO2 AIR	B MET O
		SO3 COORD	SO3 OPS	SO3 AIR OPS	
		SO3 PROG	SO3 TRG	SO3 AIR TRG/DOC	
		SO3 RES	SO3 TRG AIDS	BFSO*	
		SO3 SCHED	SO3 RANGES	BATCO	SO3 MIL

ARMD	ARTY	INF	TAC	TRG SP	FD MOB
DEPT	DEPT	DEPT	DEPT	GP	GP
LCol	LCol	LCol	LCol	Maj	Maj

* Direct access to COMD on
Flight Safety Matters

ADM DIV

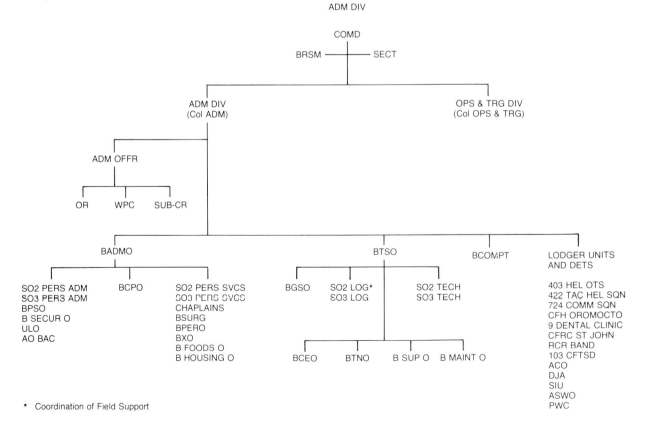

```
                    COMD
         BRSM ──────┼────── SECT
                    |
      ┌─────────────┴──────────────────┐
   ADM DIV                         OPS & TRG DIV
   (Col ADM)                       (Col OPS & TRG)
      |
   ┌──┴──┐
ADM OFFR
   ┌──┼──┐
  OR WPC SUB-CR
```

BADMO			BTSO			BCOMPT	LODGER UNITS AND DETS
SO2 PERS ADM	BCPO	SO2 PERS SVCS	BGSO	SO2 LOG*	SO2 TECH		403 HEL OTS
SO3 PERS ADM		SO3 PERS SVCS		SO3 LOG	SO3 TECH		422 TAC HEL SQN
BPSO		CHAPLAINS					724 COMM SQN
B SECUR O		BSURG					CFH OROMOCTO
ULO		BPERO					9 DENTAL CLINIC
AO BAC		BXO					CFRC ST JOHN
		B FOODS O					RCR BAND
		B HOUSING O					103 CFTSD

BCEO	BTNO	B SUP O	B MAINT O

ACO
DJA
SIU
ASWO
PWC

* Coordination of Field Support

entire Gagetown establishment under the CTC. The idea behind this action was to ensure "that a balanced and sound total support capability . . . (was) built into the base, one . . . given formal recognition and . . . guaranteed." Keystone to this realignment was the restructuring of tactics into a Tactics and Training Development Department responsible for developing, teaching, and monitoring combined arms doctrine, combat team tactics and tr ning methods. Its purpose was simply to group combat and training development activities plus tactics and doctrine (all thought to relate to one another) under experienced field officers as a method of dealing more effectively with such activities. It was to be an innovative cell, one that focussed on new combined arms tactical concepts and training methodology. The Trials and Evaluation Section, "the only army organisation established solely for the conduct of user trials on both new and in-service equipment," for obvious reasons also came under Tactics and Development.

In order to formalise this realignment, new organisation orders for Gagetown were agreed to in January, 1978, and promulgated in September. Most significantly, the combat arms departments were redesignated schools and their respective Officers Commanding elevated to Commanding Officer status accordingly. This increase in autonomy was buttressed by a further decentralisation of support resources and demonstration troops to schools: the CTC battery to Artillery School, the CTC squadron to Armour School, and the infantry demonstration and mortar platoons to Infantry School. Although a two-branch staff system of operations and administration was also provided for, the CTC staff was in practice united under a single Chief of Staff for all purposes. The evolution of the CTC thus continued.

Today the organisational structure of the CTC reflects the seventh and latest significant adjustment. Effective March 1983, Headquarters CTC returned to a two-branch staff system while including several other organisational and responsibility changes that took place after the 1978 reordering. The CTC proper is thus currently composed of Armour School, Artillery School, Infantry School, Operations Division, Tactics Division, and Training Development Division. CFB Gagetown, the garrison entity, comprises Personnel Division, Technical Services Division, and Comptroller Division. Two integral field units support training at the CTC: "C" Squadron, The Royal Canadian Dragoons, which is double-tasked as "flyover squadron" in support of its parent regiment in Germany, serves as the CTC armoured squadron; and 22 Field Squadron, which also has deployment tasks in Europe in event of war, provides engineer support. Essentially, the CTC role has remained unchanged. It is still

An infantry company halts for a brief rest and discussion during an exercise. (CFB Gagetown)

Outline Organisation (March 1983)

CTC/CFB Gagetown

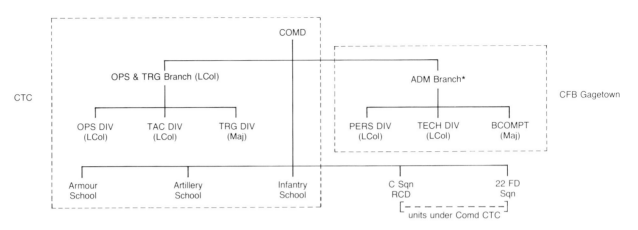

CTC

COMD

OPS & TRG Branch (LCol)

OPS DIV (LCol)   TAC DIV (LCol)   TRG DIV (Maj)

ADM Branch*

PERS DIV (LCol)   TECH DIV (LCol)   BCOMPT (Maj)

CFB Gagetown

Armour School   Artillery School   Infantry School

C Sqn RCD   22 FD Sqn

units under Comd CTC

* Deputy Commander, CTC

As a result of the study completed 1 May 1972, with the above role and functions in mind, and with an On-Site Management Evaluation Team (OSMET) reviewing the CAS organisation and establishment, the School re-designed its instructional side of the house. Changes were also made on the staff side involving mainly a sharing of responsibilities with the Staff officers at CTC Headquarters.

Live firing of the TOW missile can be done in tactical settings. (CFB Gagetown)

responsible for all combat arms leadership courses and all individual advanced technical courses for the combat arms. It is also responsible for teaching combat arms tactics at the combat team level and below. The *raison d'être* of the CTC thus remains heavily oriented toward practical combined arms training.

Within the CTC the Armour School conducts tank gunnery training, advanced driver and advanced communications training for all arms, and basic and advanced leadership courses; the school has ten Leopard tanks and a support squadron equipped with M113 and Lynx tracked and Cougar wheeled armoured vehicles. The Artillery School conducts gunnery, survey, air defence, locating and intelligence training, as well as advanced and basic leadership courses; it has on establishment a tactically organised battery of nine M109 self-propelled howitzers and nineteen 105 mm towed howitzers. The Infantry School conducts small arms, TOW and other support weapons training, in addition to a multitude of basic and advanced leadership courses. It also conducts specialist training such as sniper courses. Supporting the three schools are the CTC divisions: Operations, responsible for range and training area allocation and day to day coordination and control of all training and operational taskings; Training Development, responsible for management of training aid and production facilities, research assistance and ADP support generally; and Tactics, responsible for contributing to an disseminating doctrine, conducting combined arms training, and the trial and evaluation of weapons and equipment.

Because CFB Gagetown was originally designed to accommodate the operational training of field force formations, its use as a combat training centre proper was neither foreseen nor planned for accordingly. Recently, however, an architectural contract was let to expend roughly $70 million on the design and construction of a new training complex. It is anticipated that this major project will be completed by the summer of 1987. A complimentary and comprehensive range development plan will ensure at the same time the orderly development of training area facilities. The wisdom of choosing Gagetown for such expansion is supported by the fact that New Brunswick at its own request has been declared under the new Canadian Constitution an officially bilingual province. Though still the most conspicuously Loyalist province in Canada, its population remains approximately 40 per cent francophone. Since the move of the Francophone Training Detachment from Valcartier to Gagetown in 1978, about 26 per cent of candidates routinely undergoing training at Gagetown have been francophone, the CTC meeting their language requirements for instruction in French.

The wisdom of having a centre at which members of the combat arms train together is, of course, close to irrefutable. The German Army, at least, would appear to agree. At its *Kampftruppenschule* (Combat Arms School 2) in Münster-Lager armour, armoured reconnaissance, tank destroyer, and armoured infantry officers and men train together in what is described as a system of "course integrated leadership training at all levels." It claims to be the only school in NATO to do so. Combined arms training, if it is to be at all effective, must surely begin with a mental attitude that transcends the frequent parochialism of the single arms. Surely, too, this must be inculcated at the fighting levels. "The fact that . . . commanders are graduates of . . . Staff College and know how to use combined arms teams," according to one American officer, "doesn't mean a thing to the trigger-pullers because these senior officers won't be fighting the battle. The captains, lieutenants, and noncommissioned officers will . . . (but won't) know how because they haven't been trained!" Significantly, a major recommendation of the 2nd Battalion, The Parachute Regiment, following the Falkland's War was that "all arms training, particularly large scale live fire training, must occur more often." The Soviets, with even the basic structure of their field formations reflecting combined arms, appear to understand as much. So, evidently, do the Australians who are getting into the mechanised league and contemplating combining their single arms schools. According to MajGen J. F. C. Fuller, one's order of battle normally reflects one's order of march. The way we think we will fight in war should surely, therefore, be the way we train in peace. In this regard the Canadian army, small as it is and notwithstanding a penchant for reorganisation after reorganisation, has probably basically got it right.

Coast Defence in the 1980s

Edwin Ralph

In 1949 the United States Coast Artillery was disbanded, its weapons scrapped and its forts turned over to other military uses or converted into public parks. In 1956 the British Army followed suit, the Minister of War saying that "In the light of modern weapons development there is no justification for retaining coast artillery." Other countries pruned their defences similarly. Still other countries, however, did not, and coast defence artillery is still a viable branch of national defence in several strategically important nations around the world. There are some observers who have suggested that had the Falkland Islands held a battery of guns and a small force of gunners, history might have taken a different course.

The principal argument advanced against the retention of coast artillery was that modern missiles can simply pass over the batteries and wreak havoc at will. This was perfectly true, but it suggests a faulty analysis of the nature of warfare which was common in the immediate post-war years. Then the future was seen solely as a matter of nuclear-tipped missiles conducting war at long range, push-button warfare in which soldiers would never confront soldiers on the ground. The intervening years have shown that while this scenario still has a small amount of validity, the actual

course of warfare has tended along the well-worn grooves and that the ultimate arbiter remains a man on the ground with a rifle in his hand. And somehow that man has to get on to the territory of the enemy.

Again, reverting to the postwar years, the stock answer offered was that the enemy would use airborne forces, once more passing over the coast defences to drop well behind. But most of the major nations have now realised that overwhelming airborne attacks of this nature are no longer possible with the advanced air defence systems which are now in near-universal service. Airborne forces are now relatively small components of armies, retained for rapid deployment in limited actions where air superiority can be achieved for a long enough period to permit the force to land.

The fact remains, therefore, that to put any serious force into a sea-girt country a naval force is required, and such a force could be completely destroyed by a modern coast defence system. For such a system would no longer be dependent upon tube artillery. The Argentine defenders of Port Stanley took two Exocet missiles in their naval launch containers, welded them to a trailer, and with the very minimum of fire control managed to fire one and hit HMS *Glamorgan* some 20 km (12 miles) offshore. If such a result can be achieved by what amounts to a last-minute sticks-and-string arrangement, what might be possible with a properly equipped missile battery?

The various coast defence forces which exist today

A Bofors 75 mm rapid-fire gun in an armoured turret, one of the many modern coast defence weapons guarding Swedish shores.

Above: A battery of 5.25-in (133 mm) dual-purpose coast defence/anti-aircraft guns in "suspended animation" in Gibraltar. This is probably the only 5.25-in battery left in existence and the guns are no longer in functioning order.

Below: An Exocet anti-ship missile being fired from a shipboard mounting.

A mobile land-based Exocet launcher, carrying four missiles, in its firing position. Equipments such as these can be rapidly brought into action at any threatened point on the coastline.

(so far as are known – some countries never mention them) indicate that the missile is being given pride of place in the battle order, particularly among the oil-rich countries of the Middle East. In Scandinavia, where Norway and Sweden still have considerable amounts of coast defence weaponry, the gun is still predominant, largely because once a coast gun is installed it can stay in place for years without losing any of its potency as a deterrent. It is believed that the Norwegians, for example, still man some defence guns which were installed by the Germans during their occupation of 1940–45, their efficiency having been upgraded by the addition of modern radar fire control equipment. Similarly the Yugoslavian coastline is protected by ex-German weapons, plus a number of more modern equipments. In Sweden modern rapid-fire guns in armoured turrets which appear to have been influenced by modern tank technology are located in positions giving command of likely landing points.

Spain and Portugal, together with Turkey, were the inheritors of much of the British Empire coast defences when they were dismantled in the late 1950s; 6-in (152 mm) and 9.2-in (233 mm) guns from Britain went to Portugal, and several 9.2-in from Canada went to Turkey, while twin-barrelled six-pounder (57 mm) anti-torpedo-boat guns from Canada are still in position guarding Norwegian harbours. Spain is believed to still have a number of 12-in (305 mm) guns bought from Britain prior to the First World War; the guns may be old, but the 850 lb (386 kg) shell is still capable of devastating a warship at 32 km (20 miles) range.

But it is the missile which is now coming to dominate the coast defence world. Yugoslavia, Poland, the Soviet Union, Cuba and Egypt are all known to deploy quantities of the Soviet *Samlet* cruise missile from both fixed locations and in mobile batteries which can be moved rapidly to any threatened point. *Samlet* is an air-breathing jet-propelled winged missile with a range of possibly 200 km (124 miles) at Mach 0.9, and it relies upon radar control to take it to the general area of the target, whereupon it turns to its own radar homing head to provide the terminal guidance phase of its flight. The Soviets also use the *Sepal* cruise missile, which is a special coast defence version of the *Shaddock* shipborne weapon. This is a very large winged missile, launched from a mobile transporter, with a range of 450 km (280 miles). Guidance is by radio command, with mid-course guidance provided by patrol aircraft or ships, and with active radar homing for the terminal phase. Each Soviet coast defence battalion is said to be equipped with between 15 and 18 of these missiles.

The French, and several other nations, have adopted the land-based Exocet missile as their coast defence weapon. Mounted on a special wheeled transporter-launcher which carries four missiles, Exocet is a "fire-and-forget" weapon which, once given a target which has been acquired by the battery's radar, is simply launched and left to its own devices. If the target is over the horizon, then a patrol aircraft can perform the target acquisition and relay it to the missile as it passes. Exocet has a range of 70 km (43.5 miles), and the sinkings in the South Atlantic have shown that it is quite capable of dealing with a modern warship.

The Norwegian coast defence force has adopted the "Penguin" missile, originally a ship-borne weapon, in either fixed or mobile configuration. "Penguin" is smaller than Exocet and has a range of only 30 km (18.6 miles), but its 120 kg (265 lb) warhead is sufficient to do severe damage.

Sweden has adapted the RB 08 shipborne cruise missile to coast defence, though little has been made public of this application. This missile is a winged device based on a target drone airframe, adapted to carry the warhead and guidance system. The range is believed to be in the region of 250 km (155 miles), carrying a 250 kg (551 lb) warhead, and the weapon is guided by initial aiming, an autopilot, and active radar homing.

A British Sea Dart missile being launched from a ship: It requires little imagination to see how such a device could be land-emplaced for defence.

Even Taiwan has developed its own coast defence missile, the "Hsiung Feng," though informed opinion is that this is little more than a locally-developed variant of the Israeli "Gabriel" shipborne missile. If so it will probably have a range of about 35 km (22 miles), be given a preselected flight path on launch, and rely upon active radar homing to find its target.

Perhaps the most advanced coast defence missile system is the "Otomat," developed jointly by France and Italy, and a description of this system will give an insight into the capabilities of missiles in this role. "Otomat," as envisaged in use, would consist of several coast defence units each provided with a command group and two or four firing groups. The command group consists of a cabin truck with the fire control centre, a radar vehicle and possibly a maintenance vehicle. Each firing group would consist of a launcher vehicle with two missiles and a reload vehicle with another two missiles. All the equipment is mounted on heavy-duty cross-country wheeled vehicles, mostly of Berliet construction.

Target acquisition is performed by a Thomson-CSF search radar which passes information to the fire control centre. Several targets can be tracked simultaneously and the fire controller can select a target and, by VHF radio link, pass data to the missile launcher, program the missile for flight, and authorise the firing by the launcher crews. Once fired, the missile follows its programmed flight path, and this can be updated

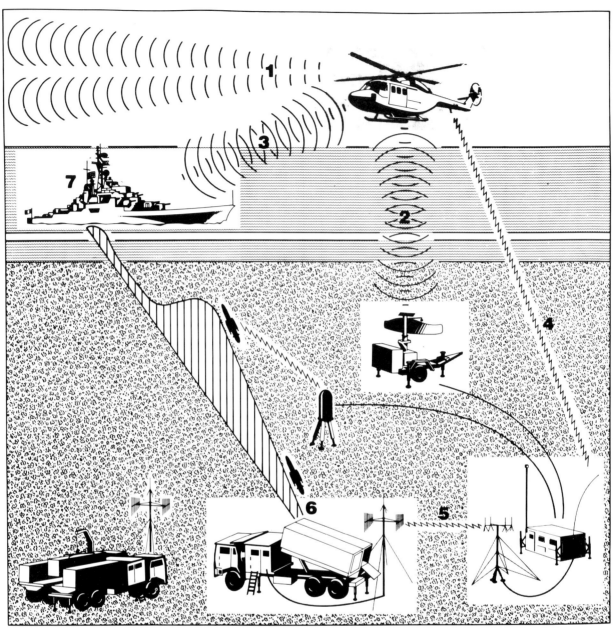

Diagram showing the operation of an "Otomat" coast defence battery. (1) the helicopter conducts a radar search whilst (2) being tracked by the ground surveillance radar. When (3) the helicopter detects the enemy ship, it (4) transmits target back to the battery. There the commander transmits firing data to the launcher (5) and orders a missile fired. The missile (6) follows its commands and finally sweeps close to the sea (7) for the terminal phase of the attack.

during flight by either the fire direction centre or by a pre-stationed helicopter or other radar carrier along the flight line. The operational range of the missile is in the region of 180 km (112 miles), and ten coast defence units can completely cover a coastline 340 km (211 miles) long, acting independently or in co-ordinated engagements.

The Egyptian Navy (who are responsible for coast defence) has purchased a number of "Otomat" coast defence units; the exact number is not known, though a total of 20 batteries has been suggested. In mid-1982 the Italian Navy were said to be considering equipping with a version mounted on tracked vehicles, and the manufacturers stated that two other countries were about to order coast defence installations.

Undoubtedly, the advent of missiles has revitalised coast defence and produced a viable and attractive method of defending a coastline once again. Perhaps the most significant feature is the mobility. No longer is it necessary to anchor the coast defence into permanent forts whose location rapidly becomes known to any potential enemy. Instead a powerful rapid-response force can be kept in readiness at any convenient and protected location, given responsibility for a stretch of

Above: An Exocet MM40 missile being launched from the mobile coast defence unit.

Below: An Otomat missile leaves its shore-based launch unit on a flight which will take no more than 6 minutes to reach a target 100 km (62 miles) away.

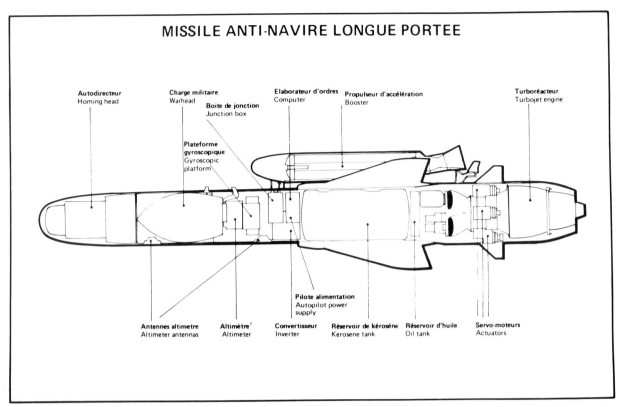

MISSILE ANTI-NAVIRE LONGUE PORTEE

Autodirecteur
Homing head

Charge militaire
Warhead

Boite de jonction
Junction box

Elaborateur d'ordres
Computer

Propulseur d'accélération
Booster

Turboréacteur
Turbojet engine

Plateforme
gyroscopique
Gyroscopic
platform

Pilote alimentation
Autopilot power
supply

Antennes altimetre
Altimeter antennas

Altimètre
Altimeter

Convertisseur
Inverter

Réservoir de kérosène
Kerosene tank

Réservoir d'huile
Oil tank

Servo-moteurs
Actuators

A diagram showing the principal components of the Otomat missile.

coastline, and turned out into a "readiness" position when danger threatens. From there it can deploy to a firing position in a very short time, acquire its target, launch a missile, and then fold its equipment and depart, entrusting the missile to find its own target and leaving nothing but an empty field for a retaliatory missile to find. This is the ideal to which railroad-mounted coast defence guns were aiming in the 1920s and 1930s, but neither their speed of response nor their flexibility were in any way comparable to today's missile batteries. Another advantage is that, as can be seen from the details given above, most of the coast defence missiles in use today are adaptations from shipboard weaponry which is already in existence and which can be converted to the land role in a relatively simple manner, so that there is no requirement for prolonged research and development programmes or expensive new equipment orders. In years gone by navies and coast defence frequently shared the same guns, the view being taken that they also shared the

same targets, and there is the possibility that missile weapons replaced in fleet service due to technical advances might well be perfectly adequate for land use for a further generation.

Another parallel with the past which comes to mind is the possibility of a dual-purpose anti-aircraft/coast defence missile. This was achieved in the days of tube artillery with the British 5.25-in (133 mm) equipment, developed in the closing year of the war and extensively installed in the 1950s, only to be removed very soon afterwards when anti-aircraft missiles took over and the coast requirement was dropped. In view of the suggestion mentioned in the opening paragraph, that a battery of guns on the Falklands might have made a great deal of difference, and the recent statements about installing anti-aircraft missile batteries there, it would appear that such a dual-purpose missile would be tailor-made for such situations.

In short, we can sum up by saying that coast defence, far from being a redundant concept retained only by backward nations in order to occupy their conscripts, is alive and well and shows every sign of making a come-back.

The Underground World of the Land Mine

T. J. Gander

The modern land mine came of age during the Second World War and ever since has been gradually developed into a fearsome and lethal weapon. But somehow it has always lacked the "sex appeal" of other more sophisticated weapon systems and the very idea of using the land mine as some form of organised booby trap weapon has led to a general dislike of the device by many, both within military circles and without. But for all that, the land mine is with us still, and today is perhaps even more important than it has ever been. It deserves a closer study than has been the norm in the past for in many ways the land mine is perhaps one of the best and most useful of all the possible counters to modern armoured warfare using formations *en masse*.

Current Use

Three recent military campaigns have once more pushed the land mine to the fore as a viable and modern defensive measure. One of these has been their use in the Falklands where Argentinian troops hurriedly sowed large minefields using untrained soldiery for the purpose and consequently not compiling logs or maps of their efforts. The resultant minefields remain uncharted in the main and their boundaries are now fenced off, rendering large areas of real estate unusable by the local populace.

Another recent campaign where land mines played a part was the Israeli advance into Lebanon in June 1982. As the Israeli armoured forces moved along the roads to Beirut just about the only obstacles they encountered

Artist's schematic of the full range of FASCAM mines in use.

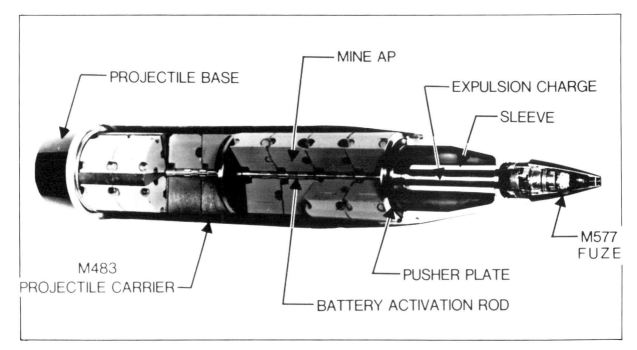

Layout of the ADAM projectile.

The Extended Range Anti-armour Mine with antennae deployed.

were land mines, some of them very simple devices indeed and some little more than explosives packed into tin boxes. Once the Israelis reached Beirut their delaying tactics had no more effect on the course of events although many remained to cause the odd nuisance incident.

The same constant nuisance effect is still being felt by the South Africans as the result of Angolan SWAPO guerillas operating inside Namibia. The guerillas have developed the art of using the land mine as a constant attacking weapon by laying them under roads near South African Army bases and consequently destroying road transport. The ploys and counter-ploys involved in this form of mine warfare are many and various but the end result is that the South Africans have to devote much of their time and facilities to the constant detection and countering of the threat. The South African forces have now been brought to the state where they have even developed special protected vehicles to at least reduce the effects of the mines but they still suffer casualties when vehicles are overturned or forced off the few roads available.

These three examples provide an indication of the use of land mines today. One is that they can prevent an enemy from using tracts of land where land mines have been sown. By denying the use of chosen areas an enemy can be channelled to other areas where the advantage will be with the defender and the subsequent levelling out of any disparity in numbers or equipment. The land mine can also purchase for a defender the one thing that he always requires, and that is valuable time. In so doing the price is paid by the attacker, for the only way to attain the maximum impact from large forces composed of modern armour is to keep them rolling onwards. Once they are forced to stop, or even slow

SKEET
SENSOR FUZED
SELF FORGING FRAGM... W.

SFFW
SELF FORGING FRAGMENT WARHEAD

**How the self-forming fragment warhead works –
a step-by-step demonstration by the AVCO company.
(I. V. Hogg)**

down, their destructive and disruptive potential is considerably reduced.

The main problem for any commander in Europe, where land mines are most likely to be used to their maximum effect in any future conflict, is that people live there and thus it is virtually impossible to have pre-sown and prepared minefields ready to meet an attack. In an emergency minefields will have to be laid in a very short time and this has led to the introduction of a whole new family of land mines generally known as FASCAMs (FAmily of SCAtterable Mines). FASCAM is an American term which should strictly be applied to their family of scattered mines only but the term is now in fairly general use to describe any grouping of mines that are dispensed by rapid methods.

FASCAMs include what are now the two main categories of mines, namely anti-tank mines and anti-personnel mines. (Current British terminology uses three categories, largely for clearing purposes, and these are non-metallic, minimum metallic and metallic). Anti-personnel mines are small and intended to injure or maim rather than destroy as the subsequent casualty handling will involve an enemy in expending facilities on transport, manpower and other expense that could otherwise be turned against the adversary. Anti-tank mines are intended to at least disable armoured vehicles – a "kill" is ideal but a disabled vehicle and its crew can take no further part in any conflict.

Early examples of these two types of land mine involved in the FASCAM concept are the British Bar Mine System and the THORN EMI Ranger System. The Bar Mine System uses a long bar-shaped anti-tank

The British Bar Mine Layer in action. With very little modification this can be used to lay the new Full Width Anti-armour Mine (FWAAM). (PR BAOR)

mine which is rapidly sown using a chute and plough assembly towed behind a FV432 armoured personnel carrier. Whole areas can be sown with Bar Mines in a surprisingly short time and the resultant furrows soon blend with the local surface conditions and become invisible from the vision devices of most armoured vehicles. The same FV432 could also carry the Ranger system which fires small anti-personnel mines from projector tubes to distribute the mines in random patterns over areas of ground. They may be spread in isolation to disable bodies of troops or they may be used spread among anti-tank minefields to hinder clearance teams.

Since the early days of the Bar Mine and Ranger development the FASCAM concept has spread to a much wider range of mine dispensing devices with the American FASCAM family proper. FASCAM now includes the Gator mine system dispensed from fast low-flying aircraft, the Universal Mine Dispensing System (UMIDS) for scattering mines from helicopters, the Ground Emplaced Mine Scattering System (GEMSS, the famous "Frisbee Flinger") using the towed M128 mine dispenser, and the Modular Pack Mine System, or MOPMS which can dispense mines from pre-placed packs that act as containers and projectors combined. There is also the M57 Anti-tank Mine Dispensing System (ATMDS), the American equivalent of the Bar Mine System, and the artillery-delivered Remote Anti-Armour Mine System, or RAAMS. With the advent of the MLRS rocket system another delivery system will be in being, adding yet another element to the overall FASCAM concept.

Above: Loading the Ranger mine-dispensing projector, seen here mounted on a Stonefield light truck. (Stonefield Ltd)

Below: Mine laying Swedish style using the FFV Minelayer.

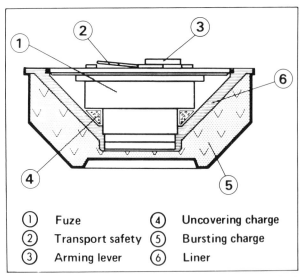

① Fuze	④ Uncovering charge
② Transport safety	⑤ Bursting charge
③ Arming lever	⑥ Liner

Cross section of the Swedish FFV 028 anti-tank mine, typical of many of its kind.

The South African Anti-tank Mine Mo. 8, typical of the new non-metallic mines.

The Soviet TM-46 anti-tank mine, a metallic mine typical of many similar types still encountered all over the world.

The German DM-11 anti-tank mine is entirely of explosive, mixed with a polyester resin to give mechanical strength. It is seen here being laid on top of an anti-lifting device. (C. F. Foss)

The Argentinian FMK-3 anti-tank mine, one of several non-metallic mines that have caused so many clearance problems in the Falkland Islands.

One of the potentially most troublesome of all types of mine, this MISAR SB-33 scatterable mine was used in large numbers in the Falklands and has proved to be almost impossible to detect by any means. It is only 88 mm in diameter but can still blow off a foot.

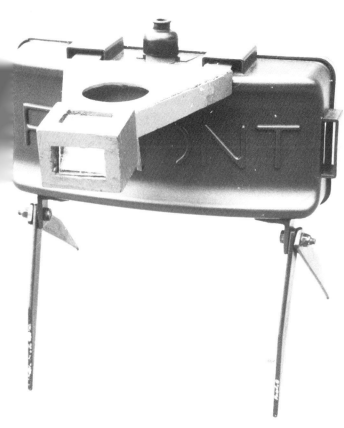

The entire FASCAM family can be used to sow mines rapidly to hamper, delay, channel and disrupt any enemy advance. But it should not be forgotten that FASCAM is only a mine delivery system and it is the mines that do all the damage. Today land mines are usually small, relatively light and packed with electronic sensors. This is a far cry from the conventional design of a large circular metal canister packed with high explosive and using a rod or pressure fuze. Many of these conventional mines are still used all over the world, a typical example being the British Mark 7 which is still in service with the British Army and may be encountered in such locations as the Indian sub-continent and has even turned up in SWAPO hands in Namibia. The Soviets have huge stocks of such mines as the TM-46 and its associated TM-57 and TM-62 and supply them liberally to their allied nations so that they too often turn up in some odd places. These metal-bodied mines will remain in use for years to come for the simple reason that they are basic enough to be used by untrained personnel and they can put up with all

The new British PADMINE seen here fitted with a model of its re-usuable Trilux aiming device.

Below: In South African border areas land mines have become such a hazard that specially protected vehicles such as this Rhino APC have been developed with additional sloped under-body armour and wire mesh over the engine to allow blast to pass through.

The Valsella SH-55 mine, used by the Italian Army, has only two metallic components, the striker point and the detonator casing. (C. F. Foss)

Left: The Soviet PMN anti-personnel mine is almost entirely of plastic and difficult to detect. It is widely used throughout the world.

Individual mines of the British Ranger system, showing the mechanical arming device which ensures that the mine does not arm until well clear of its launcher.

The Italian Valmara 69 is one of the few "bounding" mines remaining in regular service.

Below: The French "Horizontal Action" anti-tank mine can be emplaced off the road and fires a destructive shaped charge jet at its target. This picture shows a sectioned mine and also the target effect. (I. V. Hogg)

manner of rough treatment and lack of care in storage. The more recent designs have moved away from metal bodies and use plastic-based materials for the main casing. Internally metal components are kept to an absolute minimum with only such items as springs being metallic. These types of mines can be detected by sensitive detection equipments but it is a bit of a job, especially in such conditions as those prevailing in the Falkland Islands.

The FASCAM type of mines are small, sometimes to the point of being relatively ineffective against heavy vehicles. Against this can be placed the degree of design sophistication that enables small warheads to cause damage out of all proportion to their physical size. High on the list of such sophistication come the mines using the Misznay-Schardin "self-forged fragment" effect that are capable of piercing considerable thicknesses of armour using quite small detonating sources. When this destructive effect is allied with micro-electronics some of the small mines become formidable weapons. Typical of these is the American CBU-92/B submunition, part of the Extended Range Anti-armour Munition (ERAM) project. This minelet is dropped by parachute from an aircraft and once in place extends sensor antennae to detect the approach of armour. The sensors are able to sense the "signature" of heavy tanks and a micro-chip based computer in the submunition body tracks its target. It then fires a Skeet warhead at the target and automatically turns the top of the minelet

The American IRAAM remotely-delivered anti-tank mine projectile for firing from 155 mm howitzers. (I. V. Hogg)

body through 180 degrees to prepare to fire another Skeet. Each Skeet has a self-forging fragment warhead. Used in numbers these "thinking" minelets could disrupt large-scale armoured movements to a high degree, but this example is given purely to illustrate of how complex and advanced modern mine warfare has become. Other similar mine projects are in the pipeline now, and more can be expected in the future. The point has already been reached where thermal battery design can produce electronic circuits with a shelf life of over 20 years capable of powering electronic devices little bigger than wrist watches yet capable of all manner of sensor capabilities ranging from magnetic through seismic to electro-magnetic radiation detection. The degree of sophistication with some anti-tank mines of the buried type is such that in some, such as the French HPD, a small charge goes off before the main shaped charge to remove earth from the path of the destructive jet.

For all this the simple Claymore-type mines remain among the nastiest of anti-personnel weapons. In this area the American M18A1 is still one of the most widely used although the new British PADMINE and the Austrian SMI directional fragmentation mines are alternatives. The "bounding" mines are still to be encountered but these days their relative complexity and cost have tended to reduce their numbers.

Artillery-delivered mines are now one of the main development priorities in any army. One of the first in service was the Area Denial Artillery Munition, or ADAM. This cargo round (the M692 or M731) is now in US Army service and carries a load of 36 mines, each with an anti-disturbance fuzing system and a 21.25

grams warhead. Such small mines may not be able to deter concentrated tank movements but they can cause no end of second and third degree damage. Other nations are now following the American lead. The French are developing a cargo round carrying five small anti-tank mines, and the South Africans are busy developing a minelet-carrying cargo round based on their ERFB smoke projectile. The basic M483A1 projectile is now being produced by a European consortium for a variety of purposes, including mines of all types. It is almost certain that the Soviet designers are watching Western developments even if they have not yet produced their own mine-carrying projectile.

As new mines and fuze designs appear, so do their counters. If mines are sown rapidly they have to be cleared rapidly by the enemy and for this purpose even the Soviets have to employ new methods. They no longer expect leading tanks to clear minefield paths by driving across minefields these days so they equip their leading tanks with mine ploughs and rollers. The ploughs shift to one side the mines that they do not detonate and the rollers provide enough pressure to detonate anti-tank and anti-personnel mines. An alternative to these methods is the time-honoured Bangalore torpedo, but now lengths of hose are regularly delivered by rockets across minefields for subsequent filling with liquid explosive and detonation. There are numerous variations on this theme ranging from the British Giant Viper to the American Portable Mine Neutralisation System (POMINS), but one method dispenses with the filled hose altogether. This is the fuel-air explosive method in which an aerosol cloud of explosive is allowed to mix with air over a determined point and then detonated. The resultant explosion is highly productive of blast to set off any mines, but some fuzes can even defeat this drastic clearing method.

In the long run, the mines often win and have to be cleared by the old time-honoured hand clearing methods. This means probes and other such prods and a great deal of time and care, as in the Falklands. However, anti-disturbance devices of the mercury-based type make even hand clearing a very hazardous occupation and it may well be that following any future conflict vast areas of real estate will be barred from use by the presence of non-detectable mines fitted with anti-handling devices.

Plastics and nylon-based materials are now almost always used in modern mine construction so the usual metal-seeking detectors are no longer useful for the task. Sensitive "treasure-seeking" devices can detect minute amounts of metal but when a mine contains no metal the only safe way to detect it is not to even try – leave it where it is buried. Thus what may be tactical expediency in the heat of battle may well turn out to be environmental vandalism of the worst kind rendering vast tracts of country impassable to man or beast. Such large areas may be so afflicted that the long-term effect will be no less than that of serious nuclear radiation or biological warfare. There have been some conventions dealing with land mine warfare but even during relatively minor conflicts they have been disregarded and there seems to be no reason why this will not happen again.

Thus the land mine is still an important weapon. It is a sophisticated device employing modern technology at its most cunning and devious and in any future war huge numbers will be sown above and below the surface to delay, channel, hamper and disrupt. Their effect will probably be out of all proportion to their numbers and they may well have a far more important effect than many of the more glamorous weapon systems that are soaking up defence funds to such an alarming extent today. Only time will tell.

Electronic Warfare

Don Parry

Still proving highly effective, chaff systems can offer protection to a wide range of naval vessels. The photo shows the ease of loading of the new Shield decoy system which has been ordered for four new corvettes of the Brazilian Navy.

It is paradoxical that as Electronic Warfare (EW) has developed and spread across the whole sphere of military activity its definition has tended to become more and more of a generalisation.

The earliest use of EW techniques was in the disruption of communication links. Now it is used in all manner of ways and the art, for that is what it truly is, is only limited by the skill and imagination of the user. Consequently to define this type of action as denying the enemy the efficient use of his electronic systems while preserving the integrity of one's own is entirely apposite and an acceptable current definition.

EW has had a curiously cyclical history with periods of great efficiency during a conflict, then losing the expertise in times of peace only to have to undertake a painful relearning process in the opening stages of a subsequent war. This pattern has persisted from the Second World War, through Korea, Vietnam and even to the South Atlantic battles in early 1982.

A prime target for electronic countermeasures is this NATO radio relay station, here seen camouflaged in the shelter of a Second World War bunker in Holland. (HQ UK Land Forces)

There are three main applications in EW: electronic countermeasures (ECM), electronic counter-countermeasures (ECCM) and electronic support measures (ESM). ECM refers to the techniques of active disruption or interference with all types of electronic systems; ECCM is the means of countering ECM and to minimise the ability of the enemy to detect the emissions; and ESM is the use of passive techniques to support other areas of EW and to gain useful intelligence about the enemy's equipment.

A typical application of ESM would be in the use of an analyser to "listen" to enemy emissions and to determine its fundamental parameters such as frequency, pulse characteristics, pulse repetition frequency etc.

While these three basic classifications cover the major area of EW it is not entirely flippant to suggest that there is another emerging facet which may be called sociological electronic warfare (SEW). In these days of rapid, mass communication systems it can be argued that EW is practised on the social level of what used to be called the Home Front. The electronic media can present a bewildering number of options on current military tactics that can confuse and dismay many of the people who are needed to provide the strength of public opinion when confronted with the unpalatable realities of modern warfare.

While this question is more properly aimed at sociologists or moralists it can not be ignored by military realists. Anyone who spent time in the United States during the Vietnam War can have few doubts that SEW can sap the national will and eventually affect the military effort.

While progress is being made in all areas of EW there is one particular aspect that is becoming increasingly important and could provide the crucial key to military success. This is countermeasures against command, control and communication (C3) systems. Unfortunately it is also an area in which there seems to be too little international understanding and cooperation between allies. Correctly used and understood C3 is a potent force multiplier which makes optimum use of forces and limited resources. To achieve this aim it is necessary to be in receipt of large amounts of information which can be quickly processed and passed on to the relevant recipients.

The increasing use of airborne, radar and other sensors has meant that there is a very considerable increase in information now theoretically available to the force commanders. The term "theoretically" is used advisedly as it must presume that the sensors are always available in practice. Without labouring the point it

A Lynx fitted with the MIR-2 radar threat warning system. The forward-looking receiver can be seen mounted on the nose.

must be pointed out that C3 for both the British and Argentinians in the Falklands War was seriously compromised by lack of an effective airborne early warning system. This can be compared with the consummate skills deployed in this area by the Israelis in the recent war in Lebanon when outstanding victories were scored.

All this data, when it is received, must be capable of being processed properly which in turn demands the use of increasing amounts of computational power. It is all part of a need to devise a necessarily complex system that will allow gradual degradation of service under increasing enemy attack or use of electronic countermeasures. In addition it is imperative that no matter how intense the assault may be the system must still be capable of passing a certain essential, minimum traffic flow.

In the past much of the information had to be processed by manual methods of logging with much paperwork and delay involved. State boards had to be laboriously updated by hand and often the message priority was not always fully understood or appreciated. Perhaps even more importantly staff officers were reduced to the role of monitors and recorders thereby detracting from their real role of decision makers.

By comparison computers can deal with very large amounts of data extremely quickly and efficiently with an innate ability to rotate ranges of uncertainty and generate a range of options. The provision of a large data base, containing all available information on force composition and logistics, can ensure that all who have access to the system are provided with similar information which can be quickly updated allowing optimum reaction to rapidly changing tactical situations.

This data base concept allows for quick transfer of command if necessary and in the event of one element of the force moving position, it can be immediately updated and fully on-line as soon as it is established in a new position. Hard copy print-outs now replace the hand-written state sheet and the risk of fallible human intervention is kept to a minimum.

Of course it all adds to the use of electronic systems and these can be used as targets for enemy interference. This is an area of much current concern and as ever the answer seems to be a need for increasing cooperation and additional spending, neither of which tend to be too popular in the real world.

Perhaps computers do provide a degree of self-protection as they have the advantage of replacing a

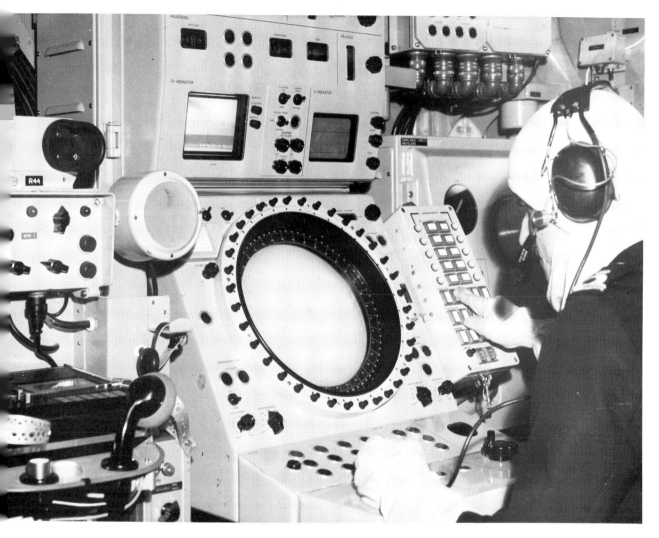

The control and display unit of the EWS-900 CA automatic chaff launcher system for FPBs and similar sized vessels.

great deal of radio traffic by use of data channels which require less bandwidth, less human intervention and are extremely fast in operation and produce completely automated updates of the formats. Data channels can be used to enhance the security and integrity of communications by the use of digitised format and high speed burst transmissions. This tends to make it difficult to detect the signal and reduce the risk of successful direction finding by the enemy. Even if the signal is detected it can endure a considerable degree of interference without loss of intelligence, unlike voice channels which are quickly degraded in the face of enemy ECM.

Other methods of improving the security can include the use of opto-isolators and fibre optic transmission links and emphasises the ever widening scope of the EW range, which in turn demands new techniques and skills as the various boundaries between the applications become increasingly blurred.

In C3 it is probably the communication element that is most at risk. It is arguably the most important as well. Voice communication is still vital and various jamming-resistant voice communication systems have been developed. Lessons learnt in Vietnam led to the development of frequency-hopping systems and for a while this type of system became something of a cult.

It is an effective method of ECCM and radios using this feature have been developed in Europe, United States, Israel and South Africa. Despite the advantages originally claimed by UK and American manufacturers the first "frequency hopper" was produced by South Africa and reportedly used in operations in the border areas. Other reports suggest similar radios were used by Argentine forces in the Falklands and examples were captured by the British.

Meanwhile manufacturers are developing new radios in which frequency-hopping is just one choice of ECCM and is offered in conjunction with other techniques. Although some reports announcing the advent of frequency-hopping as the ultimate solution gained must prominence it would be foolish in the extreme to imagine that in the fast moving science of electronics any single palliative could be pre-eminent. There are several practical ECCM techniques that are useful and helpful, though each has its own advantages and disadvantages.

For this reason it is becoming common to find designers incorporating several techniques. Computer simulation of various types of electronic attack has indicated that in the VHF bands at least there is no type of threat that cannot be countered by an intelligent combination of current ECCM techniques. This is a hopeful and encouraging sign, but in the cyclical progress of EW there are few applications that do not have a converse use.

Current research indicates that the technology used to develop frequency-hopping can be as easily applied to follower jamming systems. This opens the door to a new generation of "smart jammers" that would seem to have the ability to disrupt more than one voice communication net at a time by degrading the emission sufficiently to destroy intelligence before hopping to another net.

A Tornado fitted with the Sky Shadow ECM pod and a radar warning receiver.

Left: Technician checking an element of a computer-managed ECM system to be installed in a US Air Force B-52 bomber. (Northrop Corporation)

Certainly tactical communications are still of concern, and experience in the Falklands would suggest that numbers and deployment of such equipment should be carefully scrutinised. Perhaps this was an unconventional war in the light of modern training scenarios and there is no doubt that the need to fight a major battle more than 8000 miles from the United Kingdom was unexpected at best and somewhat unrealistic in theoretical terms.

From the beginning it was realised that communications were vital both in the tactical role and in the need to maintain and improve secure communications with the commanders and politicians in London.

In the light of available evidence it would seem that the available tactical equipment proved to work well though perhaps the availability was not always to the desired standard. It has been suggested that voices were raised against the re-equipment of some sections of the Task Force with Clansman equipment in a combination of HF and VHF equipments. The dissenters were concerned at the risk of supplying new equipment to elements more at home with earlier type radios.

It is a sentiment that can be understood, but in the

event the Clansman equipments proved to be excellent and the HF/VHF intermix proved a considerable boon in the somewhat difficult topographical conditions of the islands. Perhaps the enduring lessons that were learnt in this area are the need for compact lightweight equipment and the vital necessity of communications security (COMSEC).

Of course any consideration of the Falklands experience must take into account the rapid departure of the Task Force. In the initial stages much use was made of the ship-borne SCOT satellite terminals. Later and during the land battles long-range communication with London was maintained by TACSATCOM equipment which was placed ashore almost immediately following the initial landings.

How this pattern of command and control would have operated in the face of intense enemy electronic countermeasures is rather open to conjecture and doubtless there is much still to learn from this experience. Certainly the use of CLANSMAN radios reduced the problems of coordination between the combined forces and the use of satellite links were vital for national direction.

It has been widely reported that British monitors listened in to the airborne communications of Argentine aircraft. This was to the advantage of the British at that time though this too is a double-edged sword in more sophisticated applications. Fighter aircraft for all their sophistication still use clear voice over UHF links. This leaves them wide open to all types of electronic

interference including the introduction of spoof messages of the type that used to confuse German night fighter pilots in the Second World War.

The problem appears obvious and of long standing, though it would be wrong to suggest that nothing has been done about it to the detriment of this aspect of C3. A horrendously expensive project known as the Joint Tactical Information Distribution System (JTIDS) has been slowly developing to cover the whole spectrum of the battlefield and the air/sea components. The system uses time division multiple access techniques to allow all the computers to chatter away to each other. It is nodeless and can be fitted in ships, airborne command posts, fighters and ground systems. Each of these subscribers can receive or input data as needed. On-board equipment receives the data, decodes and displays the information and provides the converse for outgoing data. This device or terminal has been developed in three classes or sizes. Class 1 is used in the Boeing E-3A, ground stations and larger naval vessels. Class 2 is for fighter and tactical aircraft, while a projected Class 3 is expected to provide a man-portable terminal.

To date a great deal of work has been done, airline crews flying the Atlantic have been warned of possible, occasional interference to their radios during trials, and now the first terminals have been fitted in the E-3As and at least two ground stations. So far no fighter or tactical aircraft has been equipped. This is expected to take place in 1984 when tests of Class 2 terminals will begin in three F-15s.

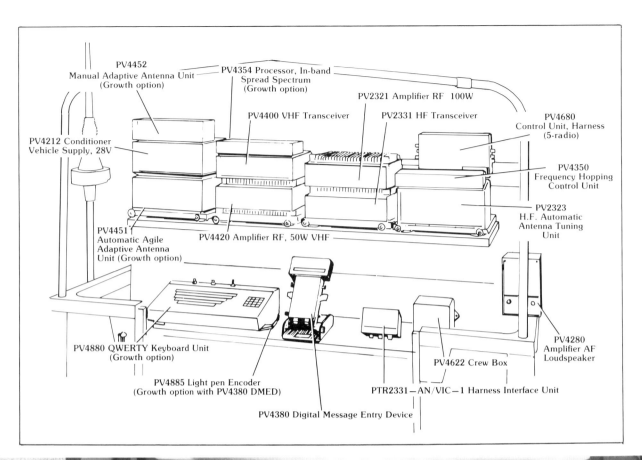

PV4452
Manual Adaptive Antenna Unit
(Growth option)

PV4354 Processor, In-band
Spread Spectrum
(Growth option)

PV2321 Amplifier RF 100W

PV4400 VHF Transceiver

PV2331 HF Transceiver

PV4680
Control Unit, Harness
(5-radio)

PV4212 Conditioner
Vehicle Supply, 28V

PV4350
Frequency Hopping
Control Unit

PV2323
H.F. Automatic
Antenna Tuning
Unit

PV4451
Automatic Agile
Adaptive Antenna
Unit (Growth option)

PV4420 Amplifier RF, 50W VHF

PV4880 QWERTY Keyboard Unit
(Growth option)

PV4280
Amplifier AF
Loudspeaker

PV4622 Crew Box

PV4885 Light pen Encoder
(Growth option with PV4380 DMED)

PTR2331—AN/VIC—1 Harness Interface Unit

PV4380 Digital Message Entry Device

Above: Thetis, an ESM system from Italy for submarines.

Left: System 4000 – a modern ECM resistant radio family seen in a mobile installation.

In 1982 NATO received the first two production Class 1 terminals and in October 1982 it was announced that an enhancement for ground based Class 1 terminals was underway with the introduction of a new system called AEGIS. This refers to Airborne Early Warning/Ground Environment Integration Segment which will eventually be installed at 42 sites ranging from Scandinavia to Turkey by the mid 1980s.

With this system radar information will be transmitted from the E-3A aircraft to existing NATO ground based command and control centres. This information will be processed and passed into the NATO Air Defence Ground Environment (NADGE) system. Meanwhile the AEW Nimrod is coming along to provide yet another valuable source of information into the C3 system.

Not so certain is the form of communication that will be used. If NADGE takes JTIDS then the AEW Nimrod must comply, similarly the RAF in general will have to follow the USAF if its choice is for the system also. It does underline the complexities in international cooperation and the problem of creating a truly secure, efficient communications system among allies.

Trends in EW are not easy to predict as many ideas

tend to fade away without realisation of expected potential while others manage to carry on for year after year; chaff is a good example of this. In general terms perhaps the most persistent trend is the continual growth in size and technical ability exhibited by the Warsaw Pact nations.

The Russians tend to refer to this branch of warfare as radio electronic combat (REC) which is their way of explaining the combination and integration of a large number of electronic functions into a single, cohesive plan that is at once both offensive and defensive.

While it is often popular, and sometimes accurate, to denigrate the technical excellence of Soviet electronics it is salutory to recall that on the two occasions that full Russian C3 has been applied it has been with total success. These events were the invasions of Czechoslovakia and Afghanistan. Once again with the Falklands fresh in mind it was the extensive use of chaff that nullified NATO radars prior to the Czechoslovakian venture. Of course this event is now some fifteen years away and it must be stressed that radar too has evolved in that time. Once again the cyclical trend appears and it is necessary to remember too that the anti-radiation missile has now emerged!

Whatever else may be argued about it does seem that in the EW role the main threats facing NATO include efficient communications, considerable expertise in deception and jamming, high resistance to ECM and mobility of C3 units.

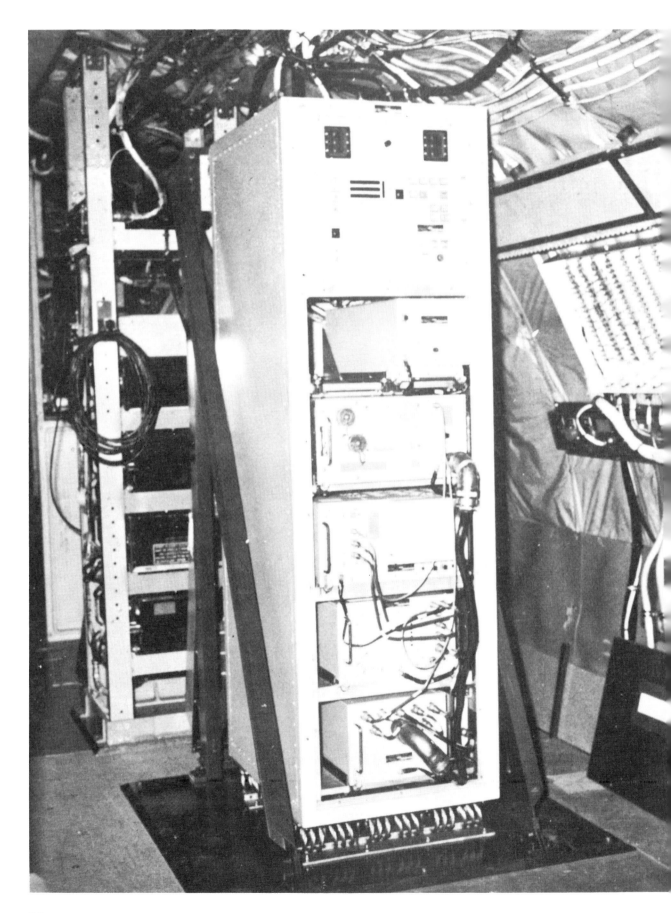

E-J BAND D-F ANTENNAS

E-J BAND DUAL RECEIVERS FORE & AFT

PROCESSOR

PILOT DISPLAY

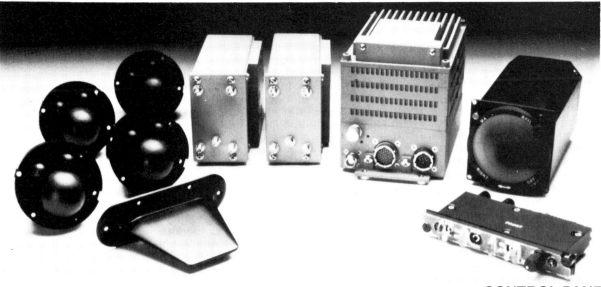

C-D BAND ANTENNA

CONTROL PANEL

Above: Katie, a modern lightweight threat warning receiver for helicopters.

Left: A class I JTIDS terminal mounted in a Boeing NKC-135.

Right: More and more military communication systems are coming to rely upon visual displays which, if fed by digitised data channels, offer considerable resistance to countermeasures. (MEL Ltd)

BA 1225

Of course each of the three services respond slightly differently to these threats. The naval concern tends to emphasise anti-ship missiles and great reliance is being placed on off-board countermeasures. Currently considerable time and money is being used in this area.

Control of own emissions is another area for concern. Radar and radio operation can easily betray the presence of naval forces, and it is likely that infra red systems will become increasingly important. Probably one of the more intractable problems is the fact that a vessel is a relatively compact unit that has to carry a great deal of electronic equipment. Mutual compatibility is not always easy to achieve and even a minor problem of interference that is acceptable in peacetime can seriously interfere with other systems in time of conflict.

In the main it can be said that until comparatively recent times land forces have been somewhat neglectful of electronic considerations. This has now changed to a marked degree with new guided missiles systems, electro-optical devices and battlefield radars. Improved communciations and the use of computer management techniques have further stimulated the army's interest in the electronic battlefield.

Now millimetric techniques are adding a further dimension and the rapid advances in electro optics are making army commanders more aware of the capabilities of electronic systems. Laser guided weapons are adding a new "bulls eye" dimension and the British Army's use of laser target designation in the closing hours of the Falklands conflict proved to be outstandingly successful.

In many minds the role of EW is synonymous with aircraft for it was during the Second World War that the first really widescale use of EW was carried out in the bomber streams over Europe.

The modern aircraft has to cope with a considerable electronic threat and is coming to rely increasingly on automation for detection, classification and reaction to threats. It has also become a considerable problem to find sufficient space for all the equipment and pod-mounted systems have proved popular though they reduce the amounts of stores, be it fuel or weapons, that an aircraft can carry.

Many voices suggested that with the new microelectronic systems and adaptable software a new integrated approach could be taken to providing a compact internally-mounted system. This led to the programme called Airborne Self Protection Jammer (ASPJ) in the United States which aimed to satisfy this demand.

It is outside the bounds of this article to consider the arguments that have surrounded this concept which has now emerged as the AN/ALQ-165. It will be fitted internally in US Air Force and Navy aircraft and somewhat perversely in pods in other aircraft. Applications for Army aircraft are currently under review.

The system is based upon highly flexible software for adjustments to changing threats and, hopefully, to avoid the early obsolescence which has been the previous fate of self-protection ECM systems. It is a modular concept of maximum commonality for reasons both of cost and compatibility with different airframes.

It is a remarkable example of modern electronic design and is said to be capable of handling conventional pulsed, high duty cycle pulsed, complex waveform and CW signals with signal processing capabilities to meet the most demanding of future envisaged threats.

Perhaps the most significant element of ASPJ is the ability to face these new threats by a software change rather than a hardware change. To this extent it has broken the cyclical nature of escalating hardware demands that has previously characterised EW. It has been achieved in technical terms, though it is not cheap. It does however indicate the current trend and direction of electronic warfare systems.

The Military Pistol Today

Gilmour Hill

The recent American trials in search of a new pistol to replace the Colt M1911A1 .45 weapon have focussed attention on an area which, for many years, has been sadly neglected. This tends to reflect the changing attitude towards the pistol in several armies; once upon a time it was regarded as a fighting weapon; then it slipped backwards to a point where it almost became an article of dress; and now it is making a resounding bid for revival, with all manner of improvements vying for attention.

Much of this renaissance must be due to the increasing burden of the internal security role. In the past this has been largely a police function and largely a dormant one, but the activities of terrorists and "urban guerillas" have now reached a point where police forces are having to be armed almost to infantry battalion standards and military forces are being impressed into internal security duties. When firearms are required in this role, they are most often required for short-range engagements, with very rapid responses demanded from the participants. Moreover the rise of such quick-response forces as the Special Air Service, the German GSG-9 squads and similar anti-terrorist specialists has set up a demand for a more informal style of weapon handling, better adapted to their role than the age-old military techniques which serve for conventional battle operations.

A minor amount of responsibility must also go to the commercial market for sporting and recreation; probably because of the publicity accorded to the derring-do

The Astra A-80, a new double-action pistol from Spain, offered in 9 mm Parabellum, .38 Super ACP, 7.65 mm Parabellum and .45 ACP chambering.

How to give an old design a new lease of life; the Beretta 951R
is a conversion of their 1951 pistol to fire full-automatic, using
a forward hand grip and an extended magazine.

The Beretta Model 92SB Compact, a shortened model which
was derived from the 92SB combat pistol.

The Beretta 92SB was developed with the US Army's trials in view; it features an ambidextrous safety catch and a magazine catch removed from its usual place at the heel of the butt to the "American" position behind the trigger guard.

of these anti-terrorist forces, the past five years has seen a dramatic rise in "combat pistol" competitions. These involve simulated combat situations – house-clearing, hostage-freeing, shooting around obstacles, rapid shooting at multiple targets and so on – and a course is laid out with several "problems" which the competitors run against the clock, their score being a combination of the time taken plus the results achieved in shooting. Unfortunately some of these events appear to pander to the lunatic fringe, resulting in contests which demand the agility of a trained acrobat in order to cope with totally unrealistic problems, but on the whole it has resulted in some interesting and inventive contests and a totally new appreciation of the requirements for a good combat pistol. And a potential sporting market in addition to the perceived military/security market has been enough to send a number of manufacturers to their drawing offices.

In order to appreciate what has been done, we should perhaps begin by looking at the military pistol as it emerged from the Second World War. In 1945 the British Army was still wedded to the revolver, though some special forces had adopted the Browning GP35 High-Power pistol; the American Army used the Colt M1911A1; the German Army had the Walther P-38 as standard; the Japanese had the Nambu and Model 94 automatics; the French had the Model 1935 MAS, designed by Charles Petter; the Italians used the M1934 Beretta; the Russians had the Tokarev TT-33; and the rest of the world used whatever they could lay their hands on.

The revolver-versus-automatic pistol controversy had raged for years, but, as the above listing suggests, the revolver was losing ground fast. This, though, was probably due to the fact that there was relatively little use of the pistol during the Second World War.

Battle casualties due to the pistol were rare, and one British general observed that of the forty or so pistol casualties of which he knew, all but two had been caused by the victim's companions in accidents. The most telling argument for the revolver was that it was faster into action in most conditions; there was no safety catch, and the firer merely drew the weapon and pulled the trigger. If the cartridge misfired, then he pulled again and a fresh round was brought into position and fired. Other advantages claimed for the revolver were that it could easily be seen whether or not it was loaded; did not require a magazine which was prone to distortion and malfunction; and was easy to clean and repair.

For the automatic pistol it was claimed that it carried more ammunition than the six-shot revolver; delivered a high-velocity bullet; was easier to shoot accurately; and could be re-loaded, by inserting a new magazine, faster than could the six chambers of a revolver. And as for the first shot, well, in combat the wise man carried

The Heckler & Koch P7, or PSP, developed as a police pistol. It uses an unusual firing system in which the firing pin is cocked by squeezing the front edge of the grip and released by pulling the trigger.

the automatic charged and cocked with the safety catch on, but in the event of a misfire he had to pull back the slide to clear the breech and reload, which could be fatal in a fire-fight.

Disregarding the Walther P-38 and Beretta for the moment, all the other automatics were of much the same type; they used a locked breech, had to be charged before firing by pulling the slide back, had a single-action lock in which the trigger merely released a cocked hammer, and usually held eight or nine rounds in a butt magazine. The Browning was the exception here since the magazine carried 13 rounds. The Beretta conformed to most of the above, but did not have a locked breech since it fired the low-powered 9 mm Short cartridge.

The Walther P-38 was the odd man out, since it used a double-action lock. This astonished most Allied soldiers who first met it, but considering that Walther has been making pistols with this mechanism since 1929 there was no reason why the principle should not have been well-known long before the war. What this meant in practice was that the P-38 owner loaded his magazine into the weapon, pulled back the slide and released it to chamber a round and then applied the safety catch, just like any other pistol. But in this case applying the safety catch placed a positive stop on the firing pin and then allowed the hammer to fall. When required, the owner drew the pistol, released the safety catch and pulled the trigger just like a revolver, raising and dropping the hammer to fire the first round. If the first round misfired, then he pulled again; in most cases this fired the recalcitrant cap. After the first round the weapon worked on single-action, just like any other automatic.

This feature of the P-38 was so remarked-upon after the war that one might have expected every other manufacturer to have immediately begun producing double-action pistols, but in fact hardly anyone bothered. Most military forces were quite satisfied with a single-action automatic and saw no need for such an expensive refinement. And there the matter might have rested had it not been for the needs of Continental police forces confronted with terrorists.

After analysing their needs, they decided that their pistols needed certain mechanical features; for example, a much bigger magazine than the standard eight or nine shots; a simple safety mechanism which did not slow down the actions of the shooter while he operated it; they needed pistols which could be operated equally well by left- or right handed men; they wanted the double-action feature to help speed up the important first shot; and, of course, they demanded simplicity, reliability and low initial cost.

Probably the earliest postwar double action pistol was the Smith & Wesson Model 39, which appeared in 1954. This had an alloy frame and double-action lock and was chambered for the 9 mm Parabellum car-

The SIG-Sauer P226 was developed specifically for the US pistol trials, and the makers claim it to be their best-ever product. (SIG)

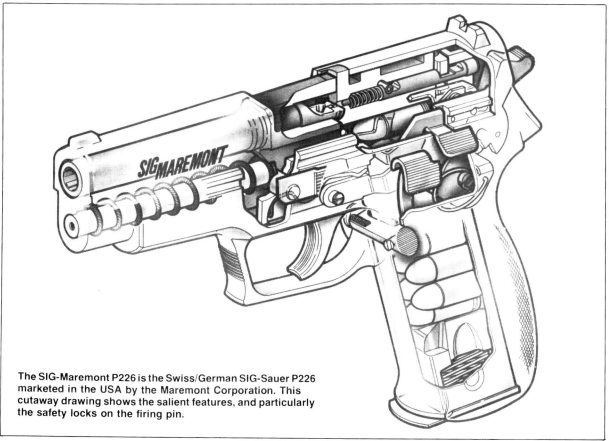

The SIG-Maremont P226 is the Swiss/German SIG-Sauer P226 marketed in the USA by the Maremont Corporation. This cutaway drawing shows the salient features, and particularly the safety locks on the firing pin.

The Astra A-90 is a newly-introduced Spanish design which incorporates double-action lockwork, a de-cocking lever, and a slide-mounted safety which locks the firing pin. Chambered for the 9 mm Parabellum cartridge, it is currently undergoing military evaluation in several countries. (Astra-Unceta y Cia)

Another new Spanish design, the Star 28DA double-action pistol in 9 mm Parabellum calibre.

tridge, and it was probably this latter feature which was responsible for its relatively listless reception. The Americans of the 1950s were quite convinced that the 9 mm Parabellum was a worthless cartridge and that nothing below .45 inch could be considered as a combat pistol round, so in spite of its virtues the Model 39 moved but slowly, and this probably inhibited other manufacturers from innovating new designs.

On the Continent, the first major step came with Heckler & Koch's introduction of the P9S and VP70 pistols in the early 1970s. The P9S, in 9 mm Parabellum, used a roller-locked breech to achieve a delayed blowback method of operation, a system based on the very successful line of military and sporting rifles which Heckler & Koch had been making for some years. It had double-action lockwork, nine rounds in the magazine, a thumb-actuated de-cocking level which allowed the internal hammer to be safely lowered on a loaded breech, and the trigger-guard shaped to suit the two-handed grip which was then coming into vogue. Altogether it was quite conventional. The VP70, on the other hand, was far from conventional and it might be said that it was this pistol which broke the barriers and made designers realise that there were other ways of making automatic pistols work than simply copying what had gone before.

The first startling feature of the VP70 was that it was largely made of plastic; the frame is of plastic with the barrel support moulded-in, and the slide is sheathed in plastic. Secondly it was a blowback weapon, something which had hitherto been considered suspect in 9 mm Parabellum chambering. Thirdly it had a magazine with the astonishing capacity of 18 rounds, yet was still so proportioned that it was possible to hold it comfortably. Fourthly it had no hammer and no safety catch; when the trigger was pulled it first cocked and then released the striker, so that unless the trigger was deliberately manipulated there was no chance of the firing pin being moved.

As if all this was not enough, the pistol came with an elaborate plastic holster-cum-shoulder stock which, when clipped into place behind the pistol, automatically activated an escapement device which allowed the firing of a three shot burst of fire for a single pressure of the trigger. This was something of an improvement on previous attempts at "machine pistols" since their principal drawback is the lack of control once automatic fire is opened; the pistol simply takes charge and, climbing high and right, sprays its shots all over the landscape. The VP70, on the other hand, fires three shots at a cyclic rate of 2200 rpm, which means that all three rounds have gone before the weapon begins to move any significant amount away from the point of aim, so that there is a good chance that all three shots will reach the area of the target.

Hard on the heels of Heckler & Koch came another

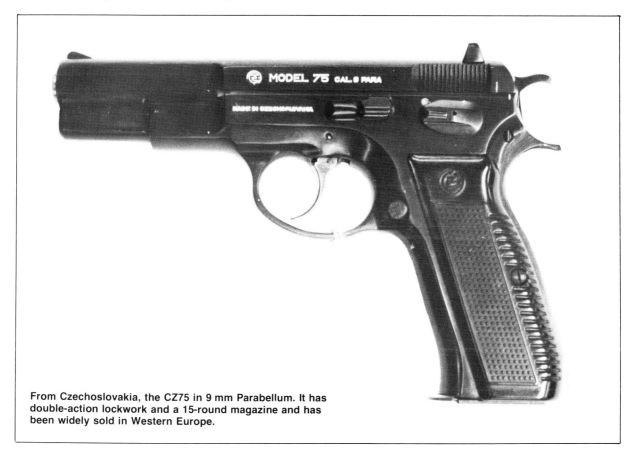

From Czechoslovakia, the CZ75 in 9 mm Parabellum. It has double-action lockwork and a 15-round magazine and has been widely sold in Western Europe.

Pistol ammunition extremes; from left to right the Soviet 5.45 mm PSM; 9 mm Makarov; 9 mm Parabellum and .45ACP cartridges.

German company, J. P. Sauer & Son of Eckernförde. Sauer had been making pistols since the 1880s, had left the firearms field in 1945 for a few years and then returned to make replica single-action "Colt" revolvers to satisfy the American "quick-draw" craze of the 1950s. In the 1970s they entered into agreement with SIG of Switzerland to manufacture SIG designs in Germany. This was simply because while SIG produced what was (and probably still is) the best automatic pistol in the world, the attitude of the Swiss government on weapon sales made it almost impossible for them to sell abroad; by, in effect, licensing their designs to Sauer for manufacture in Germany, the potential market was considerably widened.

The SIG-Sauer P220 incorporated all the modern improvements – double action lock, nine-shot magazine, trigger-guard shaped for two-handed grip, and a decocking lever which allowed the hammer to be lowered. In addition there was an automatic safety device on the firing pin which allowed the pin free movement only if the trigger was properly pulled for firing; at any other time the pin was securely locked, and therefore there was no need to fit an additional safety catch.

In 1976 Beretta of Italy introduced a series of modern pistols of which the Model 92 was the obvious military combat weapon. It incorporated double action, but without a decocking lever, relying entirely on the user lowering the hammer on to an inertia-type firing pin. The magazine contained no less than 15 rounds of 9 mm Parabellum without being too much of a handful. It was followed by the 92S which moved the safety catch from the frame to the slide and incorporated a hammer-drop action together with locking the firing pin.

There matters rested until the US Army began looking for a replacement sidearm. In the process it laid

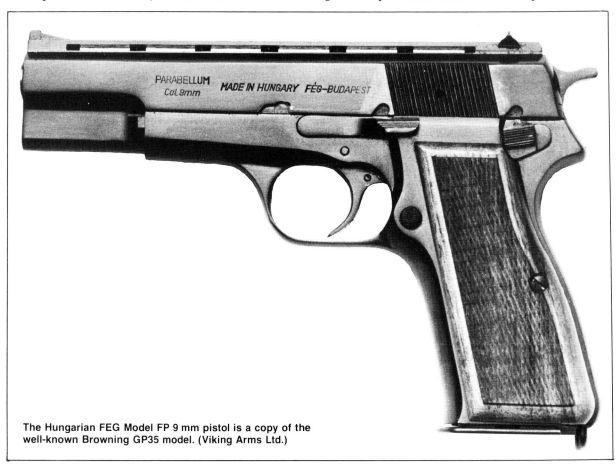

The Hungarian FEG Model FP 9 mm pistol is a copy of the well-known Browning GP35 model. (Viking Arms Ltd.)

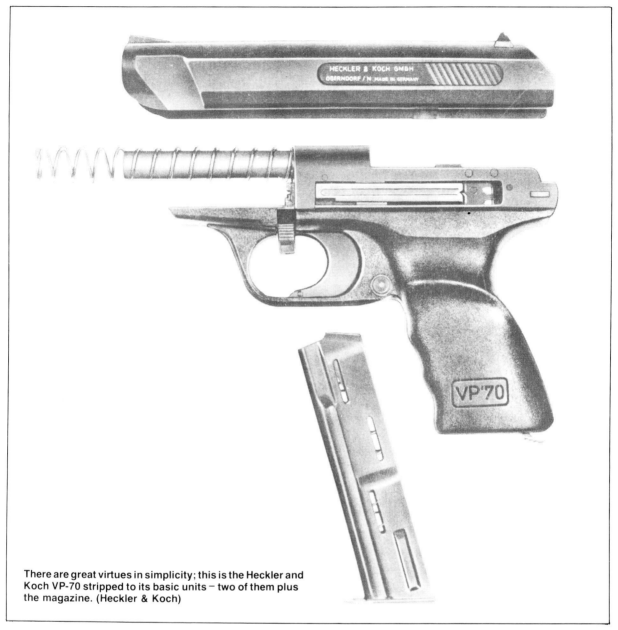

There are great virtues in simplicity; this is the Heckler and Koch VP-70 stripped to its basic units – two of them plus the magazine. (Heckler & Koch)

down some guide-lines for manufacturers, and the prospects of a major US contract were sufficient to lead to some modifications in design. Briefly the Americans wanted a safety catch which could be used by right- or left-handed shooters, and they wanted the magazine catch on the front edge of the butt, close to the trigger, rather than on the bottom of the butt which was the position favoured by most European makers. This led to the Beretta 92SB, like the 92S but with the ambidextrous safety catch and the new location for the magazine release; the SIG-Sauer P226, resembling the P220 but with an ambidextrous magazine catch; and some new arrivals such as the Star 28DA and Astra A-80 from Spain, both of which more or less conformed to the American requirement. Fabrique Nationale of Belgium, who had been quietly selling the pre-war High-

Power Browning by the thousand, now developed a double-action model, while both Colt and Smith & Wesson in the USA produced suitable 9 mm Parabellum designs; the Smith & Wesson was more or less an updated Model 39 with a 14-round magazine, while the Colt "SSP" (for Stainless Steel Pistol) has a 14 round magazine and a double-action trigger and lockwork which can be removed as a unit for cleaning or repair.

The American trials appear to have demonstrated that the Beretta design is superior to the others tested, but beyond that they have shown no firm result and there is no move to adopt any of the tested weapons in the near future. But the general consensus of design seems to have been settled; it looks as if the single-action automatic with safety catch and eight-shot magazine has definitely been superseded in military

There is still a place for the revolver; this is a Mauser design in .38 Special chambering. (Mauserwerke)

eyes by the double-action, automatic safety, 15-or-so shot magazine model.

It is noteworthy that the Americans, in drawing up their specification, appear not to have given the three-shot burst facility any consideration, and only the VP70 and a new version of the Beretta 951 model retain this principle. However, Beretta have recently introduced their Model 93R, a pistol which may, possibly, be pointing the way to the future. This resembles the 92 in general appearance but has a lengthened barrel with a muzzle compensator, a front hand grip which can be folded down, and a light metal folding stock which can be clipped to the butt to convert the weapon into a species of submachine gun. A selector switch permits the firing of three-round bursts with or without the stock attachment, and an extra-long magazine with a capacity of 20 rounds can be fitted. One weapon, therefore, does two jobs; with the standard 15-shot magazine it is a functional, if somewhat large, pistol; with the stock and larger magazine it becomes a light sub-machine gun or machine pistol, albeit restricted to three-shot bursts. The Model 93R has been adopted by the Italian Special Forces, and it will be interesting to see whether it will be more widely adopted and whether any other manufacturer will attempt to follow suit and develop a dual-purpose weapon.

And yet. Flying in the face of all this heavy-calibre equipment comes news of the newest pistol in the Soviet armoury. The Soviets have always been noted for going in their own direction, without much reference to what the rest of the world may be doing or thinking, and they have always been careful to adopt weapons which demand their own particular ammunition, even though the difference from familiar calibres may be minute – as, for example, in the case of the 9 mm Makarov and 9 mm Police cartridges which are nominally identical and yet just sufficiently different not to work in each other's weapons. But in the new "PSM" pistol the difference is so pronounced as to raise questions of just what the designer had in mind. Its calibre is 5.45 mm, and the cartridge is a bottle-necked case round of relatively low power. The pistol itself is little more than a slightly changed Makarov – which itself was no more than a slightly changed Walther PP – and the principal alteration has been the relocation of the safety catch from its usual side position on the slide to the rear, a change made, it is said, to allow the weapon to be as slender as possible for concealed carrying.

It is this latter suggestion which reveals the purpose of the pistol; it is not a combat pistol for first line troops but a concealable weapon for security forces, presumably plain-clothes men, although we are informed that it is to become the standard issue weapon for military security troops as well. But it is the low power of the weapon – it has a muzzle velocity of only 315 metres/second with a 2 gramme bullet – which invites questions about its utility. This is barely better than the .25

automatic cartridge and less powerful than the common .22 Long Rifle round. Why it was thought necessary to develop a totally new cartridge for such a weapon is beyond comprehension; the standard 7.65 mm ACP cartridge gives better performance and could easily have been accommodated in a weapon of equally small size. Perhaps the future will reveal some explanation which has not, so far, occurred to Western minds.

It may not have double-action or some of the newest safety devices, but the Browning GP35 probably arms more soldiers throughout the world than all other automatics put together. (FN Herstal)

New Equipment

Technology refuses to stand still, and there is a constant stream of new military equipment appearing all over the world. Some of it will be taken into military service, some of it may be accepted, some will vanish into obscurity, its place taken by something fresh. We present here a random selection of some of the equipment which has been announced during the past year.

Opposite: The Emerson Fast Attack Vehicle, an American proposal based on a successful cross-country racing car design. Intended to carry a crew of two and, in this case, armed with a 25 mm cannon, the FAV is envisaged as a sort of wheeled cavalry for skirmishes and raids. It has passed automotive tests and is now being given a tactical trial by the US Army.

The CETME Ameli 5.56 mm machine gun from Spain. In its early days the CETME company employed a number of Mauser technicians, so the resemblance between this and some German wartime designs is hardly coincidence. The weapon is a delayed blowback relying on the usual roller-locking system used by almost all CETME designs and perpetuated in the Heckler & Koch designs too.

Below: The Swedish Strix guided mortar bomb. It uses electro-optical seeking to detect its target and offers anti-tank performance which is usually denied to mortars. (FFV Ordnance)

Below: A Creusot-Loire tank transporter using the patented "Ampliroll" system of loading and off-loading the cargo. The platform is lifted from the chassis by hydraulic power and laid on the ground behind the truck; the tank then drives on, and the loaded platform is lifted back on to the chassis and the transporter drives off. The system has been adopted in the British and French forces for cargo vehicles but its application to tank transporters has yet to gain official acceptance.

The Jatimatic 9 mm submachine gun from Finland. Small enough to be carried in a shoulder holster (though only when fitted with a shorter magazine) and steady enough to be fired one-handed, the makers claim. Notice the angle made by the axis of the barrel with the body of the gun; due to this alignment the pistol grip is close to the axis of the recoil thrust, which helps to keep the weapon on target during automatic fire.

Left: The Centronic SAWES system for training tactical marksmanship has been adopted by the British Army. The rifle carries a lightweight eye-safe laser projectile and sight unit which, when stimulated by the firing of a blank cartridge in the rifle, "fires" a laser pulse. When this pulse strikes the detectors worn by the soldier acting as target (both "ends" of the system are seen in the picture) a buzzer sounds on the man's equipment harness and he can only stop it by lying down and taking no further part in the "battle". The system allows realistic training without danger, and has shown that even simple tactical manoeuvres can yield immense benefit when a trainees realises why and how he got "shot" and what mistakes he made.

Far Left: New anti-tank missiles are always coming along. This is the Bofors Bill, a new design from Sweden. The novelty in this design is that the missile is programmed to fly one metre above the sight line, so that if the gunner aims at the turret of the tank, the missile will fly just above it and then, by a proximity sensing device, will fire a shaped charge downward into the target, hoping thereby to find a weaker point with thinner armour than it would if fired at the side or front in the conventional manner.

Left: The German Panzerfaust 3, developed by Dynamit-Nobel, is a recoilless gun working on the countershot principle — i.e. firing a mass of plastic flakes to the rear to balance the discharge of the projectile. After shot ejection the projectile ignites its own rocket and accelerates to the target. It has a fighting range of about 350 m (1150 ft) and, when questioned, the manufacturers said that the armour penetration capability was "satisfactory". If selected to replace existing weapons, it is expected to be in production in 1985.

Below: The MIRA night sight fitted to a MILAN anti-tank missile. Developed by collaboration between TRT of France, Siemans of West Germany and Marconi of Britain, the MIRA operates in the infra-red spectrum, converting the heat of the target into a visible image which can permit the missile operator to detect a tank 3 km away and engage it at 1.5 km range. The British Army were the first NATO force to adopt the sight, placing it in service in July 1983.

Left: Lt Col Toyne-Sewell watching the inaugural firings of the Milan missile with MIRA night sight. (Ministry of Defence)

Right: The ARWEN 37 anti-riot weapon, designed by the Royal Small Arms Factory is unlikely to enter service in its original role, but may well be adapted as an infantry section close support weapon, firing anti-personnel and anti-armour ammunition. (Ministry of Defence)

The Galil sniping rifle in 7.62 mm NATO calibre. Based on the well-tried Galil rifle action, it uses a heavy barrel with a muzzle brake and is capable of a high degree of accuracy. In this picture the buttstock is folded for convenience in carrying. (IMI)

Below: A SIBMAS armoured car from Belgium, armed with a Cockerill 90 mm gun. This is probably one of the first pictures to show an amphibious armoured car firing a major-calibre gun whilst actually swimming and so demonstrating its stability. After SIBMAS showed how it could be done, everybody with an armoured car has followed suit, but we think they deserve credit for being the first.

The "AP/AV 700 Multiple Launcher",
an idea from an Italian
consortium formed by Luigi Franchi
and Misar Spa. It is a spigot
launcher which can fire three
rocket-assisted rifle grenades
and can be carried as an infantry
weapon or fitted to vehicles or
small boats. In essence, the spigot
is a NATO-standard grenade launcher
with a breech mechanism into which
a standard ball cartridge can be loaded;
versions in 5.56 mm and 7.62 mm have been made. The
grenade is slipped over the launcher and the round is
fired; the bullet is trapped in the grenade tail unit
and the gas from the cartridge launches the air, where its
rocket ignites and propels it to the target. It has a range of
700 m (2300 ft) and quite surprising accuracy.

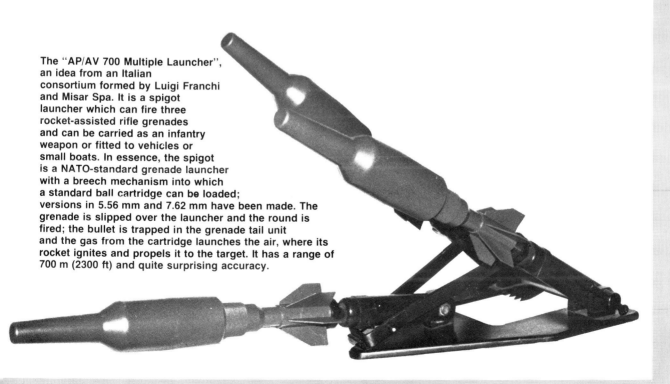

Above: The Multiple Launch Rocket System which should enter service with the British and US Armies during 1984. (Vought Corporation)

Above right: The AM-General Hummer which has been selected as the new US Army "High Mobility Multi-purpose Wheeled Vehicle" to replace the Jeep and several other light tactical vehicles over the next few years. Over 59 000 will be purchased, for about $1.2 billon, and they will be configured as weapons carriers, cargo carriers, personnel vehicles, ambulances, and (seen here) as a TOW missile carrier.

Right: A British tank firing off a screen of special smoke. Developed by Schermuly, this smoke is capable of blinding infra-red detectors, so protecting the tank against attack by missiles. (Schermuly)

Below: The new French AMX40 main battle tank. This has been designed as a potential export item, though it is possible that the French Army may show some interest. Its principal differences from the service AMX30 lie in a longer wheelbase and a new 120 mm gun.

Low-Intensity Conflict and US Special Operation Forces: Challenge and Response

David C. Isby

The 1980s have brought renewed US interest in low-intensity conflict. They have also brought about a corresponding interest in those forces that are best suited to taking part in such conflicts, namely special operations forces. This new emphasis was also in large part a result of the disastrous failure of the most recent American special operation, the abortive hostage rescue attempt in Iran in 1980. Almost four years after this defeat, much still has to be resolved regarding the challenge of low-intensity conflict and the American politico-military response to it.

The US military – especially the Army – is by no means ignorant of the importance of low-intensity conflict and the serious threat it poses to the security of the United States and of the Western world. It has stressed this threat in its 1983 briefings and testimony before the US Congress. A massive, seven-volume report commissioned by the Army and entitled *Strategic Requirements for the Army* that appeared in 1983, stated "low-intensity conflict," ranging from psychological warfare to high-tech terrorism to Soviet-backed revolutions and proxy wars "will constitute the greatest challenge to the Army." The areas of this threat are global. The report continues "In the Americas, the Soviet Union, working through Cuba and Cuban-supported proxy forces, will constitute a growing threat to vital US interests." Central America, Columbia, Venezuela and even Puerto Rico are seen as likely areas for trouble.

In a world where the strategic threat dominates by sheer destructive might, low-intensity conflict has become of necessity the instrument of choice of states or groups that intend to pursue their aims by means of arms. On a global scale, missile-armed submarines and divisions of tanks have proved successful in keeping the peace between the superpowers, but elsewhere unshaven men brandishing Kalashnikovs have toppled governments, created crises, and have managed to keep much of the world in turmoil. Nor is low-intensity conflict solely the weapon of the terrorist or the guerilla. The Soviets have an understanding and willingness to use the concepts of low-intensity conflict, directly or through proxies, as shown in Angola, Ethiopia and elsewhere. The exercise of national power in the 1980s will require both the weakest and the most powerful to project their power, and block that of their opponents, throughout the entire spectrum of conflict.

Troops from the 1/75th Ranger (Airborne) Battalion provide the Red (enemy) force on exercises in Puerto Rico. The two US Ranger battalions have no British equivalent, being a force of highly trained light airborne infantry tasked to perform missions at operational or strategic level. Unlike the British SAS or SBS, the Rangers will operate in units – battalion or company task forces – rather than special teams. The Ranger battalions have also provided many personnel for the Delta Force anti-terrorist and hostage rescue force. (US Army)

To extend the concept of deterrence – the centre of our Ptolemaic strategic universe – from strategic and theatre level to low-intensity conflict would appear to require a credible US capability to engage in, and win, such conflicts. This mandates a clear and coherent American strategy for low-intensity conflict. To make such a strategy more than rhetoric requires political will and support for the forces needed to meet a variety of threats. If deterrence is our aim, and we have certainly maintained that it is a strategic concept for a generation, then it must be realised that effective deterrence is not limited to nuclear weapons or to the balance of forces in Europe or Northeast Asia.

While low-intensity warfare has been waged throughout the world with increasing frequency in the last decade, this was not met with a corresponding American response. In the aftermath of Vietnam, low-intensity conflict became, for the American military and its policy-makers, the most unthinkable form of warfare. It was only in the last years of the Carter administration that the realisation slowly emerged that the ostrich was a poor strategic model. From this, we saw the formation of the Rapid Deployment Force and increased emphasis on the theory and practice of low-intensity conflict by the US military.

The British Army officer who once asked what the Americans were going to call the wheel the next time they re-invented it was not being cynical, for the American turnover in concepts and forces is as rapid as it is circular. "Counter-insurgency warfare" and "low-intensity conflict," the earlier phrases considered relics of the Vietnam era, have themselves been replaced by the blanket "unconventional warfare" and "foreign internal defense" (FID). Foreign Internal Defense is currently the US Department of Defense concept for operations conducted on request of a foreign government to aid allied nations attain an established level of military self-reliance. It is normally an extension of a Security Assistance Program, which means arms sales and support. Foreign Internal Defense emerged, in theory, in the late 1970s. It remains to be seen when American capabilities are to turn it into reality.

The intensity of the threat posed by the armed forces of the Soviet Union should not result in blindness (as it may have done in the United States since Vietnam) to the less dramatic but more immediate challenges of low-intensity conflict. Widespread attention has been given to the West's dependence on strategic raw materials from Third World nations, the inadequacy of stockpiles, and the insecurity of the supply of these materials. Yet the various forms of low-intensity conflict – guerilla warfare, terrorism, or invasion from bordering states (as has occurred twice in the Shaba province of Zaïre) – are probably a more real and immediate threat to the West's lifelines than even the many submarines of the Soviet navy.

The Soviets need less improvisation in doctrine to

The various versions of the Sikorsky H-53 make up much of the US Air Force's rotary-wing unconventional warfare capability. The standard special operations version is the armed HH-53E Pave Low III, fitted with armour plate and terrain-following radar. It is intended for inserting and recovering special warfare forces, usually at night and in hostile territory. Other versions of the H-53 have been used in Special Operations. Twelve CH-53C rescue ships were pressed into service to carry Marines into Koh Tang Island during the *Mayaguez* incident. The rescue ship aircrews, however, were not trained for such operations and the helicopters were not equipped with the required armament and armour. Despite the courage of the US Air Force crews, fanatical Cambodian resistance destroyed three of the helicopters and damaged the remainder. (US Air Force)

allow themselves to become involved in such conflicts. In the words of Foreign Minister Gromyko, "the Soviet people have the right to have their say in the solution of *any* question concerning the maintenance of international peace, due to the Soviet Union's reputation as a great power." The Soviets have, in the past, shown a reluctance to use force indiscriminately and have never shown any desire to force great power confrontation through low-intensity conflict. The Soviets have used their strength in this field cautiously, but they have used it well. They have used it both directly and

through proxies, but most importantly, where they have perceived that Western capabilities were lacking. Soviet opponents saw, in the 1970s, a gap between rhetoric and full confrontation in their potential responses, evidence of the absence of both a strategy and the ability to do anything in this vital area of the spectrum of conflict.

Worldwide, low-intensity conflict provides the Soviet Union with great opportunities. The superpower system means that instability serves Soviet interests, except in those areas where the Soviets perceive themselves as having the most fundamental of interests, such as Poland. Conflicts allow the Soviets to make great use of their favourite foreign policy instrument: arms sales, including the hordes of "advisors" which follow in the wake of the hardware, creating even greater internal penetration of the recipient nation. Even when the Soviets do not initiate tension or rivalries in the Third World, they can still benefit from them. The Soviets have a wide range of tactics for low-intensity conflict. They have apparently always had the will to carry them out, and this is now being matched by increasing capabilities, an explosive combination.

In any human institution, difficult decisions are normally only made when it is more difficult not to make them. In the United States defence establishment, it frequently appears that long discussions as to details are used to avoid questions about fundamentals. What the United States needs most of all at the present time is a realistic strategy for the use of military and political force and leverage in conflicts of less than global intensity and in areas elsewhere than the central front of NATO. What is needed more than weapons, more than divisions, more than warships, is thought, and it is harder to produce the thought than the hardware that should be guided by it. Today's piecemeal approaches and failure to come to grips with larger issues, it is maintained, may be disastrous if continued into the 1980s.

The most significant constraint on the formation and execution of a viable American strategy is the uncertainty of a political consensus as to the legitimacy, not only of the use of military units, but of non-military leverage as well. The tactics that the Soviets have used successfully cannot always be turned around easily, but

With his green beret and flash and his large chevrons, this Special Forces trooper dates from the 1960s heyday of Counter-Insurgency warfare. The Special Forces was originally intended to have the the primary mission of interacting with indigenous forces and host governments – in cooperation with Civil Affairs units – with the mission of commando-type special operations being secondary. In the aftermath of Vietnam, the commando-type operations became the most usually emphasised mission. The organisation of SOCOM and the existence of the Ranger battalions to handle such missions may allow more effective tasking of Special Forces assets. (US Army)

excluding their consideration as illegitimate is an exercise in self-deception that a superpower cannot afford in today's dangerous world.

An effective American strategy is really the only way to create the necessary policy stability in the Western world and, through it, what several of the essays see as a key element of any strategy for low-intensity conflicts, namely securing the trust and confidence of the governments and people involved. No nation is going to act in concert with US policy if it appears that, should the American electorate become bored with the absence of dramatic political or military success, they will find that they may be left to share the fate of the South Vietnamese or have gained nothing but international hostility for their actions.

The realities of geography and of force projection mean that the United States requires the active or passive cooperation of friendly nations if it is to assert more than a fraction of its military power potential. Yet it becomes difficult to persuade any nation to take the risks inherent in cooperating with the United States without the perception that there exists a commitment to it in return. The presence or the very existence of US military forces tailored to low-intensity conflicts will be better evidence of such a commitment than any amount of rhetoric.

It has now become apparent that reliance on regional powers, however important for American strategy, is no substitute for its absence, as the fall of Iran showed.

Yet through the 1970s, regional powers offered a comforting excuse for not evolving a strategy that would not leave the United States abdicating its responsibilities as a superpower, the same responsibilities the Soviets claim as their justification for exporting conflict. The United States would be foolish to ignore the importance of regional powers, but it has been just as foolish in believing that supporting them removes the need for planning American actions globally.

New Commands, New Capabilities

The needs of low-intensity conflict were the motivating force behind the establishment, on 1 October 1982, of the US Army's first Special Operations Command (Airborne – Provisional) at Fort Bragg. For the first time, the Army has brought all its special operations forces together under one command. This will hopefully for the first time give the US Army the ability to conceptualise the employment of such forces other than as adjuncts to heavier, conventional manoeuvre units. The inclusion of a Psychological Warfare Operations group and a Civil Affairs battalion (the only unit of this type in the active force structure) in the order of battle of first SOCOM is particularly encouraging, for experience has shown that the type of capabilities found in these units are the most valuable in many low-intensity conflict situations. Despite becoming a cynical joke in the face of the intensity of the fighting in Vietnam, "winning hearts and minds" will be crucial in just about any scenario for US involvement in a low-intensity conflict that can be imagined. The existence of first SOCOM will allow centralised and efficient

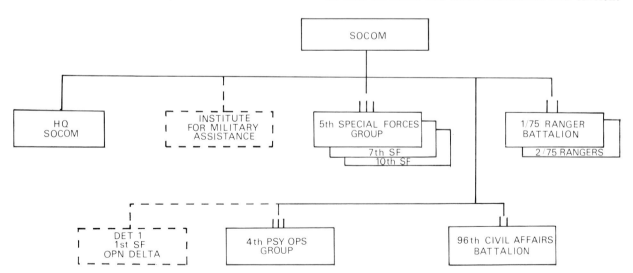

All units and headquarters are normally stationed at Fort Bragg, North Carolina, except:

10th Special Forces Group	Fort Devens, Massachusetts
3rd Battalion, 7th Special Forces Group	Panama Canal Zone (to redeploy)
1/75th Ranger Battalion	Fort Stewart, Georgia
2/75th Ranger Battalion	Fort Lewis, Washington

tasking and utilisation of the Army's special warfare assets in any low-intensity conflict. The units involved and their needs have received new attention and higher priority from the Army. Where, in the past, everything that was not oriented towards the land battle in Central Europe was made to appear redundant, today the need to respond to many possible threats with a broad range of forces can once again be considered by American planners. Clausewitz wrote "we must proportion our effort in his (the enemy's) power of resistance." If the United States has the capability of responding militarily without the masses of troops and intensive firepower that the American Way of War has traditionally required, then it is more likely to be effective.

Yet Clausewitz also wrote that war is politics continued by other means. In the wake of Vietnam, American politics have become so timid that it cannot give large-scale support to the Afghan guerillas. Even the Reagan administration has carefully limited the American presence in El Salvador to 55 unarmed training personnel, who cannot so much as swat a fly. With the passage of the War Powers Act in 1974, limiting the American President's ability to commit forces overseas and with the greater involvement of the US Congress in day-to-day foreign policy, it is obvious that the US

Special Forces troopers come ashore in an inflatable craft. Commando-type operations have always been a mission of Special Forces, and they would be tasked at Theatre or higher level. They can use conventional or nuclear demolition munitions to remove high-value targets. (US Army)

military could only be involved in an effective way in a future conflict if there was a political consensus supporting such a commitment. As very few people in American political life have any use at all for the long term, a long commitment – the very thing success in low-intensity conflict requires – will be difficult to support. Without a political consensus at home, all the capabilities of SOCOM will be impotent.

The United States does not view the challenge of low-intensity conflict as a combined effort, requiring close cooperation of the Defense Department, the State Department, the Intelligence Community (including the Central Intelligence Agency, Defense Intelligence Agency, National Security Agency, National Reconnaissance Organization, and much more) as well as the White House and the Congress. As the head of one of these bodies has stated, there is no unified policy in any given situation, and each group, ministry, or agency participating has its own independent policy. The Soviets, on the other hand, have unity of command and political-military integration as integral parts of Marxist-Leninist thought.

All of this is why, in early 1983, Colonel Charles Beckwith ("Charging Charlie" who led the Iran Raid) could still write "our Defense Department is not serious regarding special operations." Regrettably, this would appear to be the case when their application to low-intensity conflict is considered. First SOCOM is aimed at an almost infinitely wide variety of missions, from special operations in support of a major war in

Special Forces troopers move out. Napoleon wrote "An Army should have one type of infantry – good infantry" and the US military has traditionally been distrustful of elite forces. Yet without the existence of a separate force dedicated to low-intensity conflict, the demands of conventional warfare, which involve the bulk of the Army, will squeeze out the need to consider low-intensity conflict. (US Army)

Europe, to support of Rapid Deployment Force, to one-time special operations such as the Iran Raid, to long, sustained military assistance and foreign internal defense efforts. Whether one headquarters can prepare for all these eventualities is uncertain. First SOCOM does not control even the Army's reserve special warfare assets, which in some categories outnumber the regulars. But the greatest failing is that there exists no single headquarters that could integrate the forces of all services for low-intensity combat.

The United States has had problems with coordinating the efforts of its services in the past. The debacles of the Iran Raid in 1980 and the *Mayaguez* incident in 1975 were in large part due to the difficulties of co-ordinating different services that demanded to be involved. In a low-intensity conflict scenario, one might wish to involve not only forces from Army SOCOM, but the US Air Force's First Special Operations Wing, with its AC-130 gunships, MC-130 special

Armed with 105 mm, 40 mm and 20 mm cannon and a broad range of sensors and communication equipment, this AC-130H gunship of the US Air Force's First Special Operations Wing is a powerful weapon for low-intensity operations. Along with a variety of other special-purpose versions of the Hercules transport (EC-130 electronic warfare aircraft, MC-130 special warfare and command aircraft), AC-130Hs were committed to support the abortive Iran Raid in 1980. The AC-130's strongest points are its armament and sensors that enable it to destroy point targets at night, its weakest point is it vulnerability to air defence weapons. This one has four ALQ-87 jamming pods and chaff rockets. Shrouding of its exhausts have reduced but not eliminated vulnerability to SA-7 *Grail* man-portable heat-seeking surface-to-air missiles. (US Air Force)

warfare aircraft, CH-53 helicopters, and Special Operations Weather Teams; the Navy with its SEALs, Underwater Demolition Teams, and patrol craft units; and the Marine Corps with its reconnaissance battalions and companies. While US doctrine advises the establishment of *ad hoc* Joint Unconventional Warfare task forces for specific operations, these task forces are

like trying to forge a sword by gluing pieces of the finest steel together.

The US is still lacking in its approach to low-intensity conflict. Its most important lack is that of a political consensus that such conflict is at all legitimate. It also lacks the type of forces that many levels of low-intensity conflict demand. The creation of first SOCOM is obviously a step in the right direction, but until it is matched by a higher-level, multi-service equivalent, and until some degree of specialisation and specificity is possible in mission tasking, the US still cannot be said to have the forces needed to meet the challenge of low-intensity conflict. But then, with the political will and coordination absent, even the best organised forces would be helpless to affect the situation on the battlefield.

This US Army "briefing graphic" is intended to show the US Congress the Army's perception that the probability of low-intensity conflict is greater than any other kind – the trade-off being that the risks are less. (US Army)

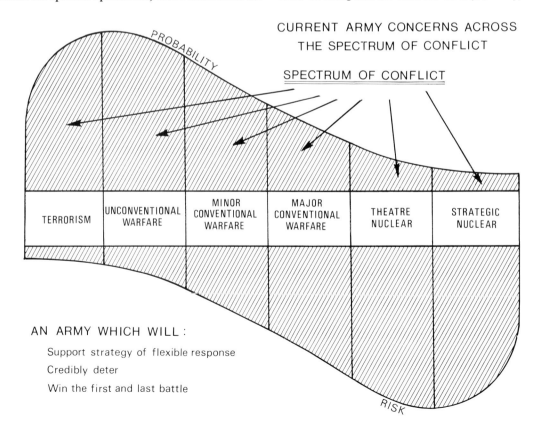

CURRENT ARMY CONCERNS ACROSS
THE SPECTRUM OF CONFLICT

SPECTRUM OF CONFLICT

PROBABILITY

| TERRORISM | UNCONVENTIONAL WARFARE | MINOR CONVENTIONAL WARFARE | MAJOR CONVENTIONAL WARFARE | THEATRE NUCLEAR | STRATEGIC NUCLEAR |

AN ARMY WHICH WILL :

Support strategy of flexible response

Credibly deter

Win the first and last battle

RISK

Military Helicopters

Michael J. Gething*

An Aérospatiale SA342 Gazelle launching a HOT ATGW on trials. (Euromissile)

The value of the helicopter to the Army Commander was brought home to the British public most effectively during the Falklands conflict in 1982. The American public had learned the same lesson during the Vietnam War. Considering that the rotary-wing branch of aviation only really began its development in the late 1930s (for the purpose of this article we are ignoring the autogyro, though we must admit that it did prove a valuable half-way house between the fixed-wing aircraft and the helicopter), the military commander has found the helicopter valuable across the whole spectrum of air operations. The Army commander used his helicopters for reconnaissance, liaison, communications, assault, troop transport, cargo transport, casualty (or medical) evacuation, anti-armour warfare, gunship duties and mine-laying. To round off the roles of today's military helicopters let us record that they are also used for anti-submarine warfare, anti-surface vessel operations, search and rescue, airborne mine countermeasures and, following experience gained in the South Atlantic, we now see an airborne early warning helicopter in operational use.

Today there are 11 major manufacturers of helicopters in the world: Aérospatiale of France; Messerschmitt-Bölkow-Blohm (MBB) of West Germany; Agusta of Italy; Kamov and Mil in the USSR; Westland in the UK; and Bell, Boeing-Vertol, Hughes, Kaman and Sikorsky in the USA. (There are also three smaller, independent, companies manufacturing helicopters in the USA but they have not been put to military use, so far as this writer is aware.)

A further 11 countries have helicopter industries based on licensed-manufacture of products from the major companies above. These are RACA of Argentina (making the Hughes 500); Helibras of Brazil (Aérospatiale Lama and Ecureil); Boeing of Canada (CH113/A Labrador/Voyageur); China, which produces license-built versions of Soviet designs plus the Aérospatiale SA365N Dauphin 2 and some new designs; HAL of India (Aérospatiale Lama and Alouette III, plus a new light helicopter of local design); P.T. Nurtanio of Indonesia (Aérospatiale Puma and MBB Bo 105); Breda Nardi (Hughes 300/500) and Elicotteri Meridionali (Boeing-Vertol

---

* Michael J. Gething is the Editor of *Defence* and a well-known aviation writer.

Above: **This model shows the tandem configuration of the Agusta A.129 Mangusta attack helicopter, armed with eight TOW ATGWs. (Agusta SpA)**

Below: **One of the A.109s captured from the Argentine Army during the Falklands campaign. Note the rocket and gun pods on the aircraft. (MJG/Defence)**

110

A British Army Air Corps Lynx AH.1 launching a TOW ATGW on trials. (Westland Helicopters Ltd)

Chinook) both of Italy; Fuji (Bell 204/205) and Kawasaki (Boeing-Vertol 107 and Hughes 500) of Japan; KAL of South Korea (Hughes 500); PADC of Pakistan (MBB Bo 105); WSK-PZL of Poland (Mil Mi-2 and the local W-3 derivative); and ICA of Romania (Aérospatiale SA316 and Puma).

Finally, there are two major international cooperative ventures presently under way; Agusta and Westland have formed E. H. Industries to develop the EH101 as a replacement for the Sea King, while MBB and Kawasaki have come together to produce the BK117.

To go further into the products of the various companies would be to present the reader with a catalogue which he is quite able to acquire from other *Jane's* publications. The above information serves merely to set the scene so far as the spread of equipment is concerned. If a country with a need for military helicopters does not have its own industry (in whatever form) then, depending upon the political sphere of influence to which it adheres and the economic deal offered by the manufacturer, he will look to his "big league" sponsor for recommendations.

Before delving deeper into the hardware which is available today, and the trends for the future, it is interesting to record the two major organisational ways in which armies receive their helicopter support. Almost without exception most major Western nations have an integral army aviation organisation. Most of these countries, and notably the USA, France and West Germany, leave all rotary-wing operations in support of land forces firmly in the hands of this army element. However, some countries, such as Britain, split the support of land forces between the army aviation element and the Air Force. Other countries either use air force aircrew to fly their "army" helicopters, as in the Netherlands, or we find that the "Air Force" is actually a branch of the army, as is the case in Austria and Eire. This division of responsibility is the subject of intense debate whenever army aviators meet, and indeed there are those who would like to see the army aviation organisations take over fixed-wing close air support duties as well as the rotary-wing ones.

Turning now to the equipment, military helicopters divide themselves reasonably easily into four main types: armed and attack helicopters, utility types, light observation types, and medium/heavy lift machines. We will consider them under these headings.

111

The latest proposed configuration for the Lynx, known as Lynx 3, shows a wheeled undercarriage, nose- and mast-mounted sights, eight Hellfire ATGWs, four Stinger AAMs, and an improved composite rotor design. (Westland Helicopters Ltd)

Armed and Attack Helicopters

Once helicopters had been introduced into the battle-field environment it was but a short step to mounting light and medium machine guns on them, to be used for keeping enemy heads down during heli-borne assaults. Armed helicopter experiments continued throughout the 1950s, but it was not until the 1960s that the true armed helicopter entered the army's order of battle. Initially, utility types were armed with various combinations of guns, rockets and grenade launchers, but following American experience in Vietnam the attack helicopter as we know it today gradually emerged. Sometimes called the "gunship," Bell's AH-1G was the first true attack helicopter; and since the US Army's code-word for armed missions in those days was "Cobra", the AH-1 series became known as Cobras or Huey-Cobras (the latter commemorating the genesis from the UH-1 Huey series of machines).

The current production model is the Bell Helicopter Textron AH-1S "Modernised" Cobra. The initial AH-1G armament of one 7.62 mm machine gun and one 40 mm grenade launcher, plus stub pylons for the carriage of rocket pods, has been progressively updated to bring in the 20 mm M197 Gatling gun (with provi-

sion for a three-barrel 30 mm cannon in the future) and provision for eight TOW (Tube-launched, Optically-tracked, Wire-guided) ATGW (Anti-tank guided weapons). The Cobra's role today is specifically against armoured targets. In the event of an armoured break-through the anti-armour helicopter is intended to provide an instant counter to the threat, in concert with ground forces and close air support (which in US terms means the A-10 Thunderbolt II with a 30 mm rapid-fire cannon using depleted-uranium ammunition and a variety of "smart" weapons).

The latest American "gunship" is the Hughes Helicopters AH-64A Apache, selected after competitive evaluation under the US Army's Advanced Attack Helicopter programme in December 1976, and now beginning series production. The Apache is a twin-engined, two-seat machine armed with a 30 mm M203E "Chain Gun©," a weapon which was also developed by the Hughes organisation. Its stub wings carry four weapons pylons which can carry either 16 Rockwell "Hellfire" "fire-and-forget" ATGWs or four 2.75-in rocket pods, or a combination of both. The main sensors for weapon aiming consist of the Martin-Marietta TADS/PNVS (Target Acquisition and Designation System/Pilot's Night Vision System) mounted in the nose of the helicopter; and the Honeywell IHADSS (Integrated Helmet and Display Sighting System) worn by the two crew members. Crashworthiness and combat survivability are prime requirements of the Apache and these have been carefully built-in: the entire structure is designed to withstand hits from any type of ammunition up to 23 mm in calibre. The US Army has stated a requirement for 536 Apaches, which will be the high technology end of the "high-low" mix of attack helicopters. The AH-1S forms the low end of the mix, and these will be available in greater numbers.

The Soviet Union's principal attack helicopter is the Mil Mi-24 *Hind* series, which has come into public prominence due to its use against guerillas opposing the Soviet occupation of Afghanistan. It was initially developed in the 1960s as a helicopter capable of delivering an eight-man assault squad into action and thereafter providing them with close air support. To this end the first three variants, code-named *Hind-A*, *-B* and *-C* respectively by NATO, had a large glass-house type

forward cockpit area. The two most recent models, *Hind-D* and *-E*, feature a re-designed twin-canopy cockpit for pilot and gunner, while retaining the cabin area in the fuselage. The *Hind-D* is armed with a 23 mm cannon in an under-nose turret, plus stub wings with four pylons able to carry gun or rocket pods or bombs, and four missile launchers for the AT-6 *Spiral* ATGW. A laser tracker and low-light TV are also mounted in the nose, and it is expected that active laser target designation systems and FLIR (forward-looking infra-red) will be added in future models. First identified in the West in 1974, it is probably the most formidable attack helicopter in service today.

Strange as it may seem, the Cobra, Apache and *Hind* are the only pure attack helicopters flying today. Two more projects, however, are in the offing; the Agusta A.129 Mangusta from Italy, derived from experience with the A.109 utility helicopter and which is expected to make its maiden flight in September 1983; and the Franco-German HAC/PAH-2 project. This has been in a stop-go situation for several years, but during the 1983 Paris Air Show it was announced that the Defence Ministers of the two countries had agreed in principle to the project going ahead. We await further developments with interest.

The armed helicopter is a slightly different animal to

The *Heeresflieger* PAH-1, a Bo 105P armed with six HOT ATGWs aimed from a roof-mounted sight. (MBB)

The Soviet Union's Mil Mi-24 *Hind-D* in Czech markings. Note the weapons pylons, nose-mounted gun and FLIR sensors. (via MJG/Defence)

the attack helicopter, and the class can be split into two basic categories: types which have been adapted to take weapons and carry them as a permanent fit for the attack role (particularly for anti-armour duties), and those types which are able to "bolt on" weapons pylons and carry podded systems to provide suppressive fire for specific operations. For our purposes we can ignore the utility machines which simply carry a pintle-mounted medium machine gun for the purpose of keeping enemy heads down during a mission.

Among the first category is the Westland Lynx AH-1; all but three of the 114 on order for the British Army are to be equipped with roof-mounted sights and eight TOW ATGWs for the anti-armour role. Similarly

the French Aérospatiale SA342M Gazelle is equipped with either four or six HOT ATGW, while West Germany's MBB Bo 105P or PAH-1 (*Panzerabwehr Hubschrauber* – anti-tank helicopter) has six HOT missiles. Both types are also adaptable to the TOW system if required. The Soviet Union's Mil Mi-8 *Hip-E*, described by the US Department of Defense as "the world's most heavily armed helicopter" with six pylons plus four launch rails for AT-2 *Swatter* ATGW also fits into this category. In the United States, Hughes Helicopters offer their 500MD Defender version of the OH-6 Cayuse as a lightweight attack helicopter with a nose-mounted sight and four TOW ATGW, while Bell have launched an armed version of their Model 206L Long Ranger armed with eight TOW ATGW under the name Texas Ranger.

Helicopters in the second category are dealt with below.

Utility Helicopters

Perhaps the most famous in this category is Bell's UH-1 Huey series, officially named Iroquois in American service, which became familiar to the world's press during the Vietnam War. It has sold worldwide and despite its place now being taken, so far as the US Army is concerned, by Sikorsky's UH-60A Blackhawk, it will be a familiar sight for many years to come. The UH-1 began life in 1955 and has been through several major developments, culminating in the Model 214ST, and has been license-built in Italy and Japan.

The UH-1's successor, as we have said, is the UH-60A Blackhawk, which began life as the Utility Tactical Transport Aircraft System (UTTAS) in 1972 and for which Sikorsky's design was selected for production in 1976. With a clean sheet of paper to work on, Sikorsky produced a Huey for the 1980s, taking advantage of all the technical developments available, such as composite structures, elastomeric rotor head and advanced aerodynamic features. The resulting machine is a more able helicopter with a crashworthy structure, capable of carrying out a full range of missions, and it has spawned four derivatives to date. A recent addition capability is the External Stores Support System, consisting of two stub wings with two stores stations on each. These can be used to carry long range fuel tanks, a variety of weapons including up to 16 Hellfire missiles, and even a scout motorcycle. According to one Blackhawk "driver" of the US Army's 101st Airborne Division "The UH-60 can carry more payload faster and further than the UH-1. Its comfort and handling greatly decreases the strain on the crew." Although only two sales have been made outside the United States at the time of writing, to

The latest Soviet heavy lift helicopter, seen in civilian markings at the 1981 Paris Air Show, is the Mil Mi-26 *Halo*. (MJG/Defence)

Above: Currently the standard US Army anti-armour attack helicopter, the Bell AH-1S Cobra is seen in its "modernised" configuration with eight TOW ATGWs, a nose-mounted 20 mm cannon and flat-plate canopy (to reduce "glint" from the sun). (MJG/Defence)

The ubiquitous Huey, seen here in the UH-1B guise, operating in the medevac role over Vietnam. (Bell Helicopter Textron)

Switzerland and the Philippines, the Blackhawk looks destined to follow the Huey around the world.

In the Soviet Union there is no true stablemate to the Huey or the Blackhawk, though the Mi-8 *Hip* may be said to take the slot, while the earlier Mi-4 *Hound* may still be seen in Third World countries. The French Aérospatiale SA330 Puma (co-produced with West-land) and the developed AS332 Super Puma have had worldwide success while the slightly smaller AS365 Dauphin 2 has yet to make a firm impact on the military market. The same may be said for Westland's W30 military variant, which has been derived from the Lynx and uses that machine's dynamic systems and engines. Another Westland development (from their Sea King anti-submarine helicopter) is the Commando troop transport which has found favour in the Middle East and, in a half-navalised form, with the UK's Fleet Air Arm as a commando helicopter operating alongside the venerable Wessex (itself derived from the Sikorsky S-58) as the Sea King HC-4.

At the lower end of the utility spectrum is the elderly Aérospatiale Alouette III, a seven-seat multi-purpose machine which has seen three "lives." Began in the late 1950s with an Artouste engine, a second life came in 1967 with the Astazou turbo-shaft engine, while its third life is with HAL in India where the SA319B Chetak version is in production. The Alouette III has sold worldwide, with over 1500 being produced.

Similar in size and role to the Alouette III but unfortunately not nearly as successful in terms of sales, is the Westland Scout AH-1. Derived from the Saunders-Roe P.351, which split into two similar types the Scout and the naval Wasp, the major customer was the British Army who used them to good effect during the Falklands campaign. Like the Alouette III with the French Army, the Scout was one of the first-generation anti-tank helicopters, fitted with a roof sight and four SS-11 ATGWs.

Light Observation Helicopters

Perhaps the classic light observation helicopter (LOH) is the Bell 47 Sioux which for ten years until 1983 introduced the M★A★S★H television comedy. Its use and deployment is, of course, much larger and widespread than devotees of the TV series may have appreciated. It has been around since 1946, though most surviving examples of the 6200 or more built are

of the later 47-G or -J models. Built under licence in Japan, Italy and Britain, the Sioux is instantly recognisable by its perspex dome of a crew compartment, looking for all the world like a flying tadpole.

Another LOH of almost equal fame is the Aérospatiale Alouette II, smaller relative of the Alouette III. Introduced into service in 1957, the Alouette II is in worldwide service and some 1300 were built. HAL of

One of the five development CH-47D Chinooks, with an underslung M198 155 mm howitzer. (Boeing Vertol)

Right: Looking like a Praying Mantis is the US Army's latest attack helicopter, the AH-64A Apache, armed with Hellfire missiles and two 2.75-in (70 mm) rocket pods. (Hughes Helicopters Inc)

India have developed and produced the "Alouette II½" – the airframe of the II with the engine and transmission of the III – known as the SA315 Lama. The successor to the Alouette II is the SA341/342 Gazelle, which features an enclosed tail rotor, known as a "Fenestron." A highly successful design, it was one of three helicopters which were the subject of the Anglo-French agreement of 1967 (the others being the SA330 Puma and the Westland WG13 Lynx). Curiously enough, the SA342 armed with six HOT ATGWs is the current French second-generation anti-tank helicopter. With typical French thoroughness, the Gazelle is well-established in the world market.

Bell's follow-on to the Model 47 was the Model 206, otherwise known as the JetRanger or, in US Army nomenclature, as the OH-58 Kiowa. Nearly 3000 of these JetRangers (including Agusta licence-built models) are in service around the world. The US Army are upgrading many of their OH-58As to "D" configuration under the AHIP (Army Helicopter Improvement Program), with four-bladed rotors, new cockpit instrumentation, a mast-mounted sight, and Stinger IR-seeking air-to-air missiles for self-defence. A close

Above: Now replacing the Huey in US Army service is the UH-60A Blackhawk, seen here embarking troops of the 101st Airborne Division on exercise. (Sikorsky Aircraft)

Right: The US Marine Corps' latest heavy lift helicopter is the CH-53E Super Stallion. Note the canted tail boom, seven-bladed rotor and third engine, with the intake to the side of the rotor head. (Sikorsky Aircraft)

competitor for the LOH role in the US Army was the Hughes 500MD development of their OH-6A Cayuse, used to good effect in Vietnam. Notwithstanding their failure in the LOH contest, many 500 MD Defenders have been sold to Third World armies as lightweight anti-armour helicopters or observation/utility machines.

The West German Army has some 227 MBB Bo 105M (VBH) liaison helicopters, which are similar to the PAH-1 but without armament, for the LOH role. The Soviet Union and Warsaw Pact still use the current version of the Mil Mi-2 *Hoplite* for LOH and liaison roles, although production is now concentrated in Poland at the WSK-Swidnik facility. Over 4000 *Hoplite*s have been produced in some 24 versions.

Medium/Heavy Lift Helicopters

An American CH-54B demonstrates its lifting ability by transporting a Roland anti-aircraft missile fire unit, weighing about 9070 kg (20 000 lb)

Above right: The Westland Lynx firing air-to-ground rockets. (Westland Helicopters Ltd)

Right: A French 20 mm cannon mounted in the door of a helicopter for air-to-ground firing. (A. T. Hogg)

There are six major medium/heavy lift helicopters in use today, with one new type on the horizon. France's Aérospatiale produce the SA321 Super Frelon which, though basically an anti-submarine helicopter, is capable of lifting 27–30 troops. The SA321Ja utility version serves with, among others, the Israeli and South African Defence Forces.

The Soviet Union, long the home of heavy lift machines, has several types in service including the Mi-6 *Hook* (capable of carrying 68 troops) and its Mi-10 *Harke* "flying crane" derivative. A new single-rotor aircraft, the Mi-26 *Halo* is now in production and is expected to supplement and eventually to replace the *Hooks* in service.

Still in US service is the CH-54 Skycrane from Sikorsky and the CH-46 Sea Knight from Boeing Vertol. The latter is used by the Marine Corps as an assault helicopter, while Sikorsky's CH-53D is their heavy lift helicopter. The latest version of the CH-53 is the triple-engined CH-53E Super Stallion, which is now in quantity production and Marine Corps service. It features a seven-bladed rotor and canted tail boom and can carry 55 troops.

Boeing Vertol are currently involved in producing the CH-47 Chinook for export, together with a major refurbishing programme to update most of the US Army's CH-47A, B and C models to an improved CH-47D configuration. This programme involves

Above: An unusual application for a helicopter – laying a lightweight fibre-optical cable for military ground communications. Helicopters can lay cable at speeds up to 185 km/hr (115 mph), so speeding up the deployment of interference-free networks. (ITT Corporation)

Left: US Army UH-60A Blackhawk helicopters in a simulated combat assault mission during an Army firepower demonstration at Fort Bragg, North Carolina. (Sikorsky Aircraft)

installing uprated engines, modern technology rotor blades and transmission, new cockpit instrumentation and an advanced flight control system. The one surviving RAF Chinook HC-1 to reach the Falklands proved invaluable to the Task Force and although having a nominal capacity to lift 44 troops actually lifted 81 on one occasion. The Chinook is also manufactured under licence in Italy by a consortium led by Agusta, and sales have been made to 13 countries including Australia, Canada, Italy, Iran, Egypt and Greece.

Currently under development in the UK and Italy is the E.H. Industries EH101 Sea King replacement helicopter. Although the initial role will be a naval one, it would not be surprising to find a military version is sold in the future.

A Hughes OH-6A helicopter demonstrating a new vibration-free "Higher Harmonic Control" system which promises to improve the accuracy of air-to-surface weapons by reducing the vibrations of the airframe by some 80 per cent. (Hughes Helicopters Inc)

A French Army Puma delivering a 120 mm mortar and crew into their firing position. The availability of helicopters confers a new mobility upon infantry support weapons. (Thomson-Brandt)

The Future

Helicopter technology today is taking advantage of several major developments to make helicopters more survivable in battle, safer and crashworthy. The use of composite materials is a prime example, while modern flight control systems, avionics and cockpit displays, rotor and transmission improvements are also to the fore.

In the future we can look forward to the development of tilt-rotor technology to increase speeds and payloads, offering military users more flexibility with their rotorcraft. The US services are investigating this with the Bell and Boeing Vertol under the JVX programme, while Sikorsky and Hughes Helicopters are both pushing advanced designs for the LHX project. This is a new concept for a family of helicopters in the scout, attack and utility roles, with a weight of some 3175–3630 kg (7000–8000 lb). Sikorsky's designs feature the advancing blade concept, which removes the need for a tail rotor, this being replaced by a ducted propulsive fan in the tail. Already we are seeing "fly-by-wire" control systems, and with the increasing use of composite materials in construction "fly-by-light," using fibre-optic transmission of control signals, with the fibres woven into the airframe, is not far off. In terms of making the helicopter less vulnerable to enemy attack, size is being reduced and IR suppressors are being fitted to engine exhausts.

The military helicopter is very firmly in the Army Commander's inventory. It is proving to be a versatile machine and in the future will be even more effective and valuable than it is today.

A Royal Air Force Puma delivering a 105 mm light gun during
exercises north of the Arctic Circle. (HQ UK Land Forces)

Something New from Africa

Ian V. Hogg

"Africa semper aliquid novi" said Pliny, quoting an even older Greek proverb – "There is always something new out of Africa". He, of course, was referring to the travellers' tales of fabulous monsters, but the adage still holds good.

Leaving aside the contentious political arguments and confining ourselves to bare facts, the Republic of South Africa is under siege. It is constantly being pressed on its northern borders by armed incursions of terrorists and has virtually existed in a state of war for the past fifteen or more years. In the early 1970s the African states were able to drum up support within the United Nations Organisation and apply pressure to various Western countries in order to deter them from supplying military equipment to South Africa, and in 1977 the UN passed a Resolution which enforced a total embargo on such supplies, an embargo which has since been closely monitored and lavishly funded, and which is unlikely to be lifted so long as the Soviet Union holds the power of veto.

By the early 1970s, therefore, it was obvious to the South African government that the country would have to become self-sufficient in armaments production if it was to survive. Steps towards this had already been taken; until 1964 all the military requirements of South Africa were satisfied from overseas, but in that year an "Armaments Production Board" was formed, and local assembly of equipment from imported components began. This provided a small number of companies with experience in the armaments field, and from this base the local manufacture of low-technology equipment and components was begun.

A Ratel 20 IFV gives supporting fire to an infantry section during a fire-and-movement training exercise in the Namibian bush. (A. T. Hogg)

A Ratel command vehicle, armed with a 12.7 mm machine gun, demonstrates its suspension on a vehicle test track in South Africa. (A. T. Hogg)

Later in the 1960s, with the prospect of an embargo being widely discussed, steps were taken to obtain manufacturing licences for certain basic military items such as infantry mortars, armoured cars and rifles. But while a licence gives permission to manufacture, it does not automatically bestow the necessary ability, and it became necessary to develop the industry until it was capable of making good use of the licences. South Africa, however, had a good technological base: steel-making had been indigenous since 1924, an explosives industry had been set up in the early years of the century (principally in order to serve the mining industry), automobile assembly from imported components had begun in the 1930s, and military ammunition had been made during the 1939–45 war, so the ability was there. The difficulty was bringing together sufficient skilled engineers and technicians, wooing them away from industry and motivating them to the uphill task of creating a military industrial complex virtually from scratch.

There was, though, one plus factor which made the whole task a little easier, and that was the well-defined nature of the military threat. There would be no need to

develop nuclear submarines, strategic bombers, intermediate-range ballistic missiles or similar expensive and time-consuming devices. The threat was one which could be contained and countered by the application of simple infantry and artillery weapons, armoured vehicles and light strike aircraft. But while the "shopping list" could thus be fairly closely defined, it was necessary to apply the maximum technological expertise to such relatively simple items in order to make them qualitatively superior, since there would be little hope of attaining quantitative superiority. The Soviet bloc began pouring weapons into Mozambique and Angola after the Portuguese revolution of 1974, and the South African industry was unlikely to be able to compete in a sheer numbers game.

The Research & Development phase, therefore, had a reasonably concise area in which to concentrate its efforts, but this was tempered by the peculiar conditions in which the equipment was to be employed. On the credit side there was to be a close consultation with the users of the equipment, who were extremely knowledgeable about what was required and highly reactive – if a piece of experimental equipment was given to the army, they could put it to practical test and give their conclusions in a matter of days, rather than the months which elapse in other countries. As a result of this it was soon apparent that operational requirements could be

129

rapidly identified and rapidly communicated to the R&D staffs, and that if there was no apparent requirement, then no time would be wasted in developing equipment. As one South African soldier said, "If we haven't got it, it's because we probably don't need it."

On the debit side were the climatic conditions which faced South African troops. In the first place the rainfall is low, so that less emphasis needs to be put on swimming ability in vehicles and bridging equipment. On the other hand the sand and dust of the Kalahari Basin, the existence of bush over a major portion of the country, the inhospitable coastline all demand that vehicles be built to extremely high standards of reliability since much of the logistic support of forward units must be vehicle-borne.

As a result of all these factors, the situation today is that South Africa is about 95 per cent self-sufficient in military production. It is entirely self-sufficient insofar as conception, design and development are concerned, and the five per cent which needs to come from outside is not, in fact, military equipment *per se* but tools and technical assistance, and within the foreseeable future even these will not be required. The South African arms industry has now reached the stage where it can offer its products on the world market, and the proceeds from this trading will fund the necessary research

---

Left: A Ratel 90 IFV negotiating a steep incline on the rough section of the Elandsfontein vehicle test track. (A. T. Hogg)

A Ratel 90 during a firing demonstration. (A. T. Hogg)

---

and development effort for the next generation. The industry made its first moves in this direction in late 1982 when it took a stand at the Defendory Military Exposition in Athens; this was a well-kept secret which took the defence industries of the rest of the world completely by surprise, particularly when the quality and range of South African products became apparent. Inevitably, it produced the reaction which might have been expected, and after four days the stand was closed and the exhibitors asked to leave, but they left secure in the knowledge that they had made their point. And there seems to be little doubt, though official confirmation is not forthcoming nor is ever likely to be, that the export trade is gathering momentum. What is noteworthy is that some of the customers appear to be within the African continent, which suggests that some African countries are as adept at saying one thing and doing another as were their colonial masters of yore.

Today the defence industry is headed by Armscor, the Armaments Corporation of South Africa. In simple terms, Armscor is the controlling body for a federation of companies who, between them, can produce whatever the military need. The chain of command is that the military define a requirement, Armscor examine it and farm the project out to the company or companies having the necessary expertise, giving assistance in the R&D phase as necessary. A prototype is developed and handed to the military, who test it and report their findings. The development company then makes such modifications as may be necessary in the light of the

The Ratel Logistic Vehicle, showing how the containers are fitted between the armoured crew cab and the armoured engine compartment at the rear. Note also the crane, folded across the top of containers. (A. T. Hogg)

military report, and re-submit the equipment for further tests. Once the equipment is approved, Armscor then allocate the manufacture, since it may be that the company who were adept at development may not have the facilities for mass production. Throughout the process, Armscor keep a watching eye on progress, ready to bring in expertise from elsewhere in the confederation should it be required and generally acting as midwives to the project. Where specialist machinery or plant is likely to be required, Armscor will fund the necessary construction; if specialist materials are needed, Armscor sees to the supply, and so on. And at the end of the day, when the immediate military requirement has been satisfied, Armscor will examine the export potential and look for customers.

The range of equipment now being produced under Armscor's guidance is extensive and technologically advanced. In the six years since the application of the UN embargo, a broad-based defence industry has been put together which is thoroughly up-to-date and cap-

able of manufacturing everything which the South African Defence Force requires.

Infantry are provided with the R4 rifle; this is actually the Israeli Galil with some modifications. The Galil was chosen largely because of its robustness and weight, leading to steadiness in firing and better accuracy. Even so, it was insufficiently robust to withstand operations in the South-west African bush country, and the stock has been lengthened (to better suit the stature of the South African soldier) and strengthened, being made from a carbon fibre material which is shock resistant and also does not heat up in the African sun like a metal stock.

Mortars are locally manufactured; a licence was obtained from Hotchkiss-Brandt in the early 1960s, and 60 mm, 81 mm and 120 mm mortars were manufactured. Since then, though, experience has shown where improvements might be made, and a totally indigenous 60 mm light mortar has gone into production. Mortar ammunition is also locally made, using designs which are an improvement on the original Brandt patterns. Considerable modification has been done to the percussion fuzes to improve their reliability, and more recently a proximity fuze (known as

A Buffalo mine-resistant troop carrier. Notice the shaping of the under surface to deflect blast, and the cut-outs in the armoured sides which permit the crew to use their rifles from cover. (A. T. Hogg)

"Merlin") has been developed for use with all calibres of mortar. This uses totally new circuitry, known as the "NVSD" for "Near-Vertical Slope Detection," which reduces the risk of electronic jamming and also reduces the spread in burst height so as to give highly consistent results. Electric power is provided by a turbo-generator and the fuze is unique in having frequency agility: the emitted frequency is not constant but "hops" in a random manner so that even if a jamming device was operating, it would be unlikely to be able to jam all the frequencies in use. The fact that such a fuze has been locally developed and is entering production should be sufficient proof of the technical and manufacturing standards attained in South Africa in six years.

The "front line" between South Africa and the rest of the continent stretches roughly the same distance as from London to Moscow, so that an infantry force attempting to protect it needs transport, both of the logistic kind and of the tactical kind. Tactical transport, in an area prone to mining and ambushes, means armoured personnel carriers (APCs), and where the object of movement is to carry fighting troops into action, it also means infantry fighting vehicles (IFVs). All these various demands have been met by local designs.

The APC/IFV is the Ratel, the Afrikaans name for a small but ferocious animal known in English as the "honey badger." The basic Ratel is a six-wheeled armoured vehicle which can carry a crew of three and eight fully-equipped infantrymen in some degree of comfort. Propelled by a turbo-charged diesel engine which drives through an automatic transmission, it is capable of 105 km/hr (65 mph) on the road and has an astonishing cross-country ability. Armament varies; the standard model carries a 20 mm cannon in a small turret, together with a co-axial 7.62 mm machine gun. This is known as the Ratel 20. Next comes the Ratel 60 which mounts a 60 mm gun-mortar, derived from a Hotchkiss-Brandt design, in its turret, to provide close support for the infantry. Finally there is the Ratel 90 armed with a 90 mm gun which can fire anti-tank and anti-personnel projectiles and which generally acts as the mobile artillery and anti-tank screen for patrols.

Above: A Buffalo in its natural habitat, carrying a tracking patrol through bush country in Namibia. (A. T. Hogg)

Below: A mine-resistant ambulance.

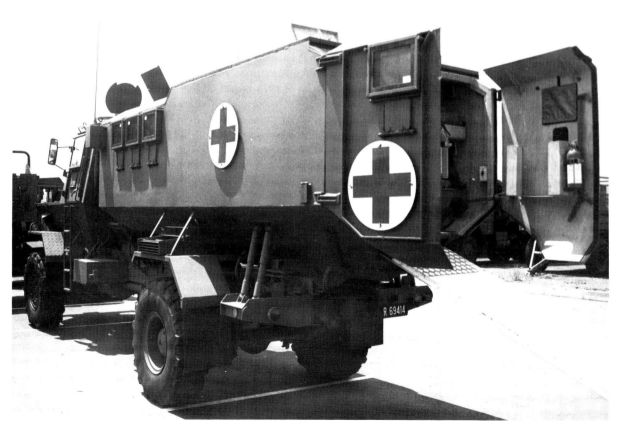

A SAMIL truck on the test track, showing how the chassis can flex over rough country. (A. T. Hogg)

The most recent addition to the Ratel family is the Logistic Ratel, which is an 8 × 8 wheeled chassis supporting an armoured cab, an armoured engine compartment, and a flat cargo bed between them. Armed only with a 12.7 mm machine gun on the cab roof, the vehicle carries a crew of three men. It has been designed to carry a selection of custom-built containers on the cargo bed, so as to function as a logistic support basc on wheels, accompanying mobile patrols mounted in the Ratel fighting vehicles. It can operate for ten days or 1500 km (932 miles) without replenishment, and carries the necessary logistic supplies for a 45-man platoon. By ringing the changes on the containers, the platoon commander can select the supplies he wishes to carry, according to the composition of his force. Thus a typical loading might be 2000 litres (440 Imp gal) of diesel fuel, 500 litres (110 Imp gal) of water, 1.5 tons of ammunition, a freezer compartment with 500 kg (1102 lb) of fresh food, plus spare wheels and vehicle spares. The vehicle carries an hydraulic crane to facilitate loading and off-loading the containers. This is the first time a vehicle has been specifically designed to provide logistic support to an armoured infantry column, and it is an excellent example of the pragmatic South African approach to their particular tactical problems.

For normal logistic supply the enormous distances involved obviously demand air assistance, but in addition a vast number of cargo vehicles are needed. A survey carried out by the South African Defence Force in the late 1960s showed that at that time there were over 200 different "soft" vehicles in use, leading to enormous problems in maintenance and spare part supply. Over 20 makes of foreign truck were purchased and evaluated, and as a result the SAMIL (South African Military) range of trucks has been developed. These have their origins in Magirus-Deutz designs, though there have been numerous modifications to suit them to operation in South Africa, where the ambient temperature can reach as high as 47°C.

Of particular interest are the range of mine-resistant vehicles, a concept pioneered in South Africa and brought to a high degree of efficiency. The vehicles have been brought into use to try and cut down the number of casualties from land mines laid by terrorists close to the Angolan border. The object has been to deflect or absorb the blast of the mine so as to preserve the occupants of the vehicle. Work began with such elementary measures as lining the vehicle floor with sandbags, filling the tyres with water and bolting on protective plates, but it progressed from this to an analysis of design features required to defeat blast. It was found that the height of the vehicle above the ground, its mass, and the shaping of the undersurface

Right: SADF gun detachment manning a G5 howitzer at the SA School of Artillery, Potchefstroom. (A. T. Hogg)

Firing the G5 howitzer at point-blank elevation. (A. T. Hogg)

into a "keel" were all inter-related, and from these studies a design evolved. Special alloys had to be developed for the protective "keel," and the design has to be carefully dimensioned so as to give ample strength without upsetting the centre of gravity. But the result is a range of special bodies mounted on 2-, 5- and 10-ton chassis which can cover every requirement, from patrol vehicles and ambulances to cargo transports. In the case of vehicles carrying personnel the entire vehicle body is shaped and protected, and the occupants are strapped in by means of four-point harness. In the case of cargo vehicles, only the driver's cab is protected, the object in view being to save lives and not to over-protect cargoes. These vehicles can drive over any conventional anti-tank mine and detonate it without ill effect to the occupants; certainly the vehicle will be damaged to some extent, but the fighting ability of the crew will not be impaired.

To support this mobile force of infantry on the frontier it is necessary to have artillery. In the past the South African Defence Force fielded a collection of ex-British 25-pounder (87.6 mm) and 5.5-in (140 mm) gun-howitzers, but excellent as these designs were even their best friends will admit that they are old. Moreover they were sadly outranged by the Soviet weapons in the

Above: The G5 self-propelled 155 mm howitzer. (A. T. Hogg)

Below: The Valkiri 127 mm field artillery multiple rocket launcher. (A. T. Hogg)

hands of Angolan and Mozambique guerilla forces. And so after examining what the artillery of the rest of the world was adopting, the SADF opted for a general-purpose 155 mm weapon capable of being employed as a gun or as a howitzer. Development began in 1976 and the resulting weapon, the 155 mm G5, is now in regular production and steadily replacing the older weapons.

The G5 is technically very advanced, at least as good as anything in the Western world and in some respects even better. A 45-calibre weapon, it has a maximum range of 30 km (18.6 miles) with conventional shell and of 37.5 km (23 miles) with a base-bleed shell. This latter is something of an achievement; several people have been working on base bleed shells for a considerable time, but the South Africans are the only army to have such a projectile in regular production and to have proved it in combat. The carriage of the gun has auxiliary propulsion, allowing the gun to be manoeuvred without needing a tractor, and the propulsion motor also provides hydraulic power for opening the trails, lowering and raising the trail dolly-wheels and powering the shell rammer.

The next step was to develop a self-propelled mounting, and for this a wheeled design was chosen. This gives better performance across the type of terrain in which the SADF operates, offers a 60 per cent reduction in fuel consumption by comparison with a tracked chassis, reduces first cost by about 50 per cent, trebles the life of the equipment and trebles the intervals between overhaul. The G6 self-propelled gun uses the same ordnance as the G5 and thus has the same ballistic performance. The current design, illustrated here, is not definitive; development is still in progress and it is anticipated that the final design will be somewhat lower and more compact and will also have automatic loading.

The last support weapon to be required was an artillery rocket, to counter the Soviet-made BM21 rockets frequently fired across the border into South African territory. The 127 mm "Valkiri" Artillery Rocket is a 24-tube launcher mounted on a Daimler-Benz Unimog 4 × 4 truck chassis. It can fire at ranges between 8 km and 24 km (5 and 15 miles), either in single rockets or in salvoes of any number up to 24. When the launch tube assembly is lowered into the bed of the truck and the canopy strapped down, the vehicle is indistinguishable from any other Unimog cargo truck.

Ratel APcs moving up behind the cover of a smoke screen fired by 81 mm mortars. (A. T. Hogg)

Behind all this lie the resources of Armscor: a barrel-making plant capable of manufacturing gun barrels up to 155 mm calibre from Electro Slag Refined steel; powder factories using the most up-to-date chemical engineering technology to produce propellant powders of unsurpassed regularity and power; electronics factories which have developed a range of proximity fuzes which in several respects are better than anything in use elsewhere in the world; pyrotechnic factories capable of producing every sort of smoke or incendiary projectile; and explosives factories filling artillery shells to the highest standards. There is little point in continuing this litany, since the point is made. Not in spite of, more because of, the UN embargo, the South Africans have not only caught up with but have, in many areas, surpassed the rest of the world in armaments development. Moreover they have achieved this in no more than seven years, and they have succeeded in their aim largely because they kept that aim limited. National security was their aim, and that is exactly what their armaments industry is geared to provide. There are lessons here for all of us.

South African Defence Force mortar detachment and 81 mm mortar undergoing training in Namibia. (A. T. Hogg)

Right: The 60 mm Commando patrol mortar developed and manufactured in South Africa. (Armscor)

Light AA Defence for Field Armies

Charles Castle

The Gepard anti-aircraft tank is probably the most expensive and complex field anti-aircraft weapon in current use. This is the Netherlands Army version, using a different surveillance radar (above the turret rear) to the German model. (Oerlikon)

Rear view of the Swiss Oerlikon twin 35 mm equipment, showing the recently-introduced ammunition resupply racks alongside the gunner's compartment. These can be loaded while the gun is in action, and their contents transferred to the gun magazines in a matter of seconds. (Oerlikon)

A report from Argentina during the Falklands Campaign spoke of their losing five aircraft "to cannon fire from the ground". If this was true, then one can only suppose that the unfortunate pilots had suffered from the attentions of their own side, for if there was one weapon which the British forces did not field it was anti-aircraft cannon. Indeed, an underlying motif of the accounts of action heard from the rank and file was the paucity of light anti-aircraft defence. As a result, as soon as an Argentine aircraft appeared, the soldiers immediately began shooting skywards with rifles, light machine guns and general-purpose machine guns. Some of this had a deterrent effect, possibly some of it had a positive effect, but for the most part the troops looked on it more as a gesture than as a likely way to bringing down aircraft. Certainly the field gunners were adamant that their issue of light machine guns was of little use for this purpose and that they wanted GPMGs in the future. The official Tables of Organisation or War Establishments provide for the ground forces to be protected by Rapier missiles as an artillery responsibility and Blowpipe missiles on a self-help

basis. Both of these performed well in the Falklands, but "there were never enough of them" is the story heard from the men who were there.

Visiting the major NATO exercise in Germany some years ago was an enlightening affair. A German Panzer squadron rumbled across the moorland, followed by a troop of Gepard self-propelled twin 35 mm guns, their turret-mounted radars scanning the skies and keeping a careful watch over the heads of the tanks in front of them. An American tank battalion followed, each cluster of M60s accompanied by a tracked Vulcan six-barrelled Gatling gun, again with its radar watching alertly. And then one saw the Royal Tank Regiment, its sleek and menacing Chieftains an impressive sight, until you realised that the only anti-aircraft protection they had was a lonely 7.62 mm machine gun stuck up on the top of the commander's cupola. Either the Army has an immense faith in rifle-calibre bullets against modern aircraft, or it has its priorities so arranged that anti-aircraft defence of moving columns is a long way down the list. Some years ago a German general pointed out that taking an armoured formation into battle without air protection was "an expensive form of suicide", but his remarks appear to have gone unnoticed.

To be fair, the root of the matter is money; a Gepard tank, probably the most luxurious of the present-day self-propelled AA weapons, costs about half as much

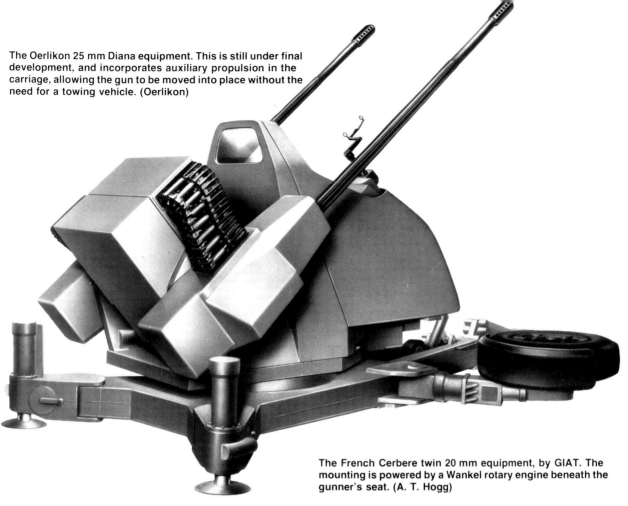

The Oerlikon 25 mm Diana equipment. This is still under final development, and incorporates auxiliary propulsion in the carriage, allowing the gun to be moved into place without the need for a towing vehicle. (Oerlikon)

The French Cerbere twin 20 mm equipment, by GIAT. The mounting is powered by a Wankel rotary engine beneath the gunner's seat. (A. T. Hogg)

The Serge Dassault TA-20 twin 20 mm turret, complete with radar and optical fire control system. (Electronique Serge Dassault)

Another French equipment, the GIAT Tarasque single-barrel 20 mm gun. Notice that the gunner is carried on the elevating mass, so that he is always in the same relationship to the sights. (GIAT)

again as a main battle tank. The US Army have recently ordered a quantity of 'Sgt York' twin 40 mm SP equipments at a cost of about six million dollars each; these are said to be an advance on Gepard insofar as they incorporate newer electronic techniques in their fire control computers which permit the prediction of curved attack courses. The Saudi Arabian government purchased a number of twin 30 mm AMX AA tanks from France some time ago at an equally fearsome price. And so long as the NATO forces in Germany suffer from a massive imbalance *vis-à-vis* the Warsaw Pact tank strength, then one supposes that the natural inclination is to spend what money is available on MBTs since they address themselves to the prime threat. But with the rise of the anti-tank helicopter, it does seem logical to think about the dangers of going into battle without the comfort of air defence. In theory the British armoured formations are to be protected by Rapier missiles, suitably deployed. But this brings up visions of Rapier batteries furiously leap-frogging along, trying to keep up with the armour, while the AA protection of the remainder of NATO moves, searches, and shoots on tracks. Tracked Rapier will shortly be deployed in Germany, but even this has to stop and take some time about making ready to fire, whereas the gun equipments can fire, with some degree of accuracy, as they move should the need arise.

But even if Tracked Rapier could operate on the move, it still seems to be an expensive form of defence against such targets as helicopters. One Rapier missile is reputed to cost £15,000, and most helicopters would succumb to one per cent of that price translated into small-calibre cannon shell. Perhaps it is time to look at some alternative methods of dealing with the sort of aerial targets likely to show up against armoured columns.

144

The Serge Dassault TA20 turret mounted on a Belgian SIBMAS armoured car. (SIBMAS)

There is no shortage of contenders for this task; most European manufacturers have addressed themselves to the anti-aircraft problem during the past five or six years. Among the most recent to appear is the Krauss-Maffei Wildcat, described as an attempt to produce a capable system at a reasonable price. The basis is a 6 × 6 wheeled armoured car, a choice which immediately helps to keep the price down, more so because the basic vehicle is already in West German army service as the Fuchs APC. On to this basic vehicle goes a turret which mounts two 30 mm Mauser Model F cannon. This is a very up-to-date weapon with dual feed (so that the gunner can switch from, say, HE shell to AP or some other type without have to stop and change belts), positively-actuated ammunition feed, a rate of fire of 800–900 rpm and a useful range of 3000 metres. The gun is chambered for the same 30 × 173 mm cartridge as is used by the USAF in their GAU-8A Gatling cannon fitted to the A-10 aircraft, so that there is no problem in procuring ammunition. Fire is controlled by a unique modular fire control system which can be put together to suit whatever particular system the customer prefers; in brief, the system offers three levels of daylight-only fire control and two of all-weather, the top-line system having a Siemens search radar, an HSA Ka-band tracking radar, an electro-optical sighting system with TV scanning, and a digital fire control computer. The entire equipment weighs 17.5 tonnes, carries 1000 rounds of ready-use ammunition, runs at 100 km/hr (62 mph) on roads, swims, and in general represents todays state-of-the-art in wheeled air defensive systems.

Unveiled at almost the same time as Wildcat was the Oerlikon GDF-CO2 tracked twin gun equipment. This, though, has a different function in life, being designed to protect fixed installations or supply columns rather than armoured formations in the front line, and to this end it is not armoured. But, again in an effort to keep the price competitive, the basis is also a well-known and widely-adopted vehicle, the US Army's M548 tracked carrier. On the rear cargo deck of this sits the Oerlikon turret, mounting two 35 mm cannon fed from 200-round externally-mounted star drums. Fire control is by a new Contraves clear weather electro-optical system comprising a periscope optical sight, laser rangefinder and passive infra-red auto-tracker. Data from this array is fed to a digital computer and gun data from there automatically aims the weapons. Only one man is required to operate the gun in action, another standing by to assist with reloading. The unit can also be cabled up to any suitable search/acquisition radar to provide an early warning facility. Weighing 16 tonnes, the GDF-CO2 is currently under evaluation by various forces.

A very similar piece of equipment has been

developed in the USA. This is the Aries Eagle, and it owes its inception to a demand put forth by the late Shah of Iran's army, who wanted a mobile defence system for vulnerable point protection. The same M548 chassis is used, and a similar turret is placed on the deck. This carried two 35 mm Talon cannon, designed by Eugene Stoner (of Armalite rifle fame), which fire the same Oerlikon ammunition as Gepard and GDF-CO2 at a rate of 600 rpm. Feed is from internally-mounted drum magazines holding 280 rounds for each gun. There is an optical sight and a laser rangefinder, feeding their data to the inevitable digital computer, and the design admits of alternative control systems being installed. In addition, the sight unit can be removed and distanced from the gun; it can also be used to control a number of gun units simultaneously. Unfortunately, by the time the Eagle was perfected, the Peacock Throne had collapsed, and it now looks like a valid solution in search of a problem.

It may yet find its niche; the German Army have stated a requirement for a new self-propelled anti-aircraft gun system based on whatever chassis eventually replaces the Marder MICV. It is to be a smaller, lighter , and cheaper vehicle than the existing Gepard, and principally intended for the engagement of helicopters. The specification calls for it to be armed

with two 35 mm guns which, though firing the same Oerlikon ammunition, must be lighter and less complex than the Oerlikon KDA cannon in Gepard. The Talon cannon weighs only 270 kg (551 lb), well below the specified limits, and the Mauser company have made some modifications to the design in order to meet German requirements and are putting it forward as the Mauser Model G cannon. Further developments will have to await the provision of a suitable chassis, since the Marder replacement has not yet been decided upon.

The Italian Army had intended to buy Gepard but cancelled the plan due to financial constraints. As a result they have no air defence vehicle, and at the end of 1979 decided to set about developing a low-cost locally-built system. OTO-Melara have produced a four-gun unit mounted on an M113A1 APC body. The guns are Oerlikon 25 mm KBA cannon, with a rate of fire of 570 rpm from each barrel. The operational analysis calls for a weapon for short range engagements (1500–1800 m/4900–5900 ft) and short bursts of fire, hence the demand for four barrels so as to deliver the maximum amount of metal to the target within a two-

Left: Soviet quadruple 23 mm guns on parade; this self-propelled equipment is widely distributed and extremely effective. (Novosti)

A battery of French twin 20 mm weapons; the centre vehicle carries the fire control radar and passes information to the others by a radio link system. (Electronique Serge Dassault)

Above: A recent development by Oerlikon is this twin 35 mm gun equipment mounted on a special wheeled cross-country chassis. It is intended as a mobile protection system for vulnerable points and field concentrations. (Oerlikon)

Below: Developed as close defence for the heavy Crotale missile batteries, this twin 20 mm weapon by Thomson-CSF is mounted on the same vehicle as used for the Crotale equipments. (Thomson-CSF)

The Krauss-Maffei Wildcat with twin 30 mm Mauser cannon, radar and optronic sights. (Krauss-Maffei)

or three-second burst. Fire control will be by means of an optical clear-weather system, using a TV tracking camera or a Thermal Imager, a laser rangefinder and an IFF system. This will auto-track the target once put on by the gunlayer, feeding data to a fire control computer which will perform the ballistic calculations and power-drive the mounting in bearing and elevation. If this all works well, then the OTO-Melara solution must look attractive to any army in need of a low-cost system.

The French have put more effort than most people into developing practical and inexpensive air defence vehicles and have several in service with foreign armies and more on offer. Much of this has been due to the availability of an extremely compact and effective turret unit incorporating a search radar, optronic sight and twin 20 mm cannon. Developed by Electronique Marcel Dassault and Panhard this TA/RA20 system is easily fitted to a variety of armoured vehicles, from four- and six-wheeled Panhard and Renault armoured cars to tracked vehicles such as the Steyr 4FK APC, the West German Marder and the ubiquitous M113 APC. These latter will also accept a heavier weapon system, the Thomson-CSF Sabre turret which mounts two 30 mm cannon together with a surveillance and range-finding radar and an optronic sight.

Enough has been said to show that there is no shortage of mobile air defence equipments, whether intended to protect a column on the move or a static vulnerable point. But it has to be admitted that these equipments, with their complex chassis and their on-carriage radar and fire control computers are still an expensive solution, both in terms of first cost and also in terms of maintenance and upkeep. This seems to have struck home in several quarters, for the past two or three years has seen a sudden rise in the number of light trailer-mounted automatic cannon.

The towed 20–25 mm gun is not new; they were being touted in the 1930s and several armies used them. But in the 1950s they fell from favour because they were *too* simple; neither their sights nor their mount-ings could cope with the faster aircraft of the day, and this, as much as anything, led to the one-man shoulder-fired missile. Now, however, advances in computing sights and the development of small engines (the Wankel rotary engine has found a useful niche here) to provide hydraulic power, have led to a number of designs which can deal very competently with today's low-level attackers.

The names of Oerlikon and Hispano-Suiza come readily to mind when light 20 mm guns are mentioned, and although Oerlikon bought out Hispano as far back as 1971 Hispano designs are still produced under the Oerlikon name. The AA equipments produced range

The Thomson-CSF Dragon, a mixture of French turret, Oerlikon 30 mm guns, and German Marder MICV chassis. The Sabre turret unit can be fitted to a variety of tank and armoured car chassis. (Thomson-CSF)

from the simple GAI-BO1 single-barrel cannon on a manually-operated mounting to a highly sophisticated twin 35 mm weapon normally used in conjunction with a full radar system. Of the light equipments, which are our concern here, the most advanced is the GAI-DO1, designed to fill the gap between the two extremes quoted above. There are two belt-fed 20 mm cannon each firing at 1050 rpm attached to a mounting which rotates above an outrigger platform, powered by a Wankel engine which provides hydraulic power for elevation and depression and electrical power for the sighting system. The sight is Italian, by Officine Galileo, and is integrated into the gunlaying system by servo-mechanisms. The gunner can feed the sight with information on target range and ammunition characteristics, and a rate gyro will determine target speed and angle, passing this information to a mini-computer. This makes the necessary calculation for aim-off and displaces the gunner's sight cross-wire accordingly. The gunner controls his weapon by a joystick and merely has to place the crosswire over the target and open fire.

The Oerlikon company's latest light weapon is a twin 25 mm equipment called Diana, and in essence it is an enlarged model of the 20 mm equipment just described, though with many improvements. The sight is a totally new electro-optical unit by Contraves, and the most innovative feature is the application of power from the engine to drive the trailer wheels so that the weapon can be manoeuvred in and out of difficult locations without requiring a towing tractor.

The French consortium GIAT (Groupement Industrielle de Armements Terrestrial) has produced a number of 20 mm equipments for service with the French Army. The latest to enter service is Tarasque, a single-barrel 20 mm cannon on a two-wheeled carriage which is light enough to be towed by any light 4 × 4 truck or slung under almost any helicopter. A small on-carriage petrol engine provides hydraulic power for elevation, traverse and gun-cocking. The cannon has dual feed, magazines holding belts of 100 rounds of HE-Incendiary shells for air engagements and 40 rounds of APDS for anti-tank ground shooting. The cyclic rate of fire is 750 rpm, and the whole equipment, in the firing position, weighs only 650 kg (1433 lb). As well as being provided in trailer form it is easily adaptable to fitting on to the cargo bed of any suitable 2-tonne truck.

Above: One of several private ventures from French makers is this Renault VAB 6 × 6 armoured personnel carrier mounting the Dassault TA/RA 20 twin 20 mm system. (Electronique Serge Dassault)

Below: Another Renault project is this VAB 4 × 4 APC with a radar-controlled short range surface-to-air missile system. The missile is the Mistral, based on that used with the French man-portable SATCP equipment. (Electronique Serge Dassault)

The German Army has years of experience with 20 mm cannon, and over 1000 of their current weapon, a twin 20 mm developed by Rheinmetall, are in service. This is a power-driven mounting on a wheeled trailer carrying two Rh202 gas-actuated automatic cannon which each have a rate of fire of 1000 rpm. The guns are single-fed, belt fed, and 560 rounds are carried on the mounting. The sight is the Italian Officine Galileo P56, as used by some Oerlikon designs, an optical sight with rate gyro prediction and a microcomputer to produce the necessary future target information. Not only do the German Army use this weapon, but it has also been supplied to the Norwegian, Argentine and Greek armies, and the French Air Force have adopted a version which substitutes French GIAT cannon for the Rheinmetall guns.

It would be possible to cover several more pages tabulating light anti-aircraft guns – for example, the Israeli Army has made a highly successful conversion of the old American twin .50 Browning machine gun mount by substituting two Hispano-Suiza 20 mm cannon for the machine guns, and with this weapon they claim to have shot down over 60 per cent of the aircraft destroyed by ground fire in the Yom Kippur War of 1973. But we think the point has been made; there is no shortage of equipment designs – what is needed is the decision to put it into service.

Another project aimed at using existing weapons in a more mobile form is the American Lightweight Chaparral which takes the missiles from their existing armoured and tracked carrier and puts them on a small air-portable trailer. (A. T. Hogg)

Opposite: The Blowpipe missile. Whilst the Falklands campaign undoubtedly proved the efficiency of this weapon, it also showed that the scale of issue and the distribution needs to be re-thought. (Short Brothers Ltd)

In the next ten years the helicopter is going to assume more importance than ever before, and largely as an attack weapon, both against tanks and light armoured vehicles and also against troops. Although the helicopter may look vulnerable, experience shows that it is not so easy to shoot down as the layman might imagine, and it is certainly not going to be put off its stroke by haphazard rifle and machine gun fire from the ground. Specialist forms of attack demand specialist forms of defence, and unless the NATO armies begin to think more seriously about the quantity of air defence, instead of concentrating purely on the quality of individual equipments, operations in the field will be put an unnecessary risk.

Remotely Piloted Vehicles

Don Parry

The military use of remotely piloted vehicles (RPVs) is one of those classically simple concepts that seem much harder to translate into actual practice. The idea has been around for a long time and several attempts have been made to use the RPVs in a variety of roles. Once or twice it appeared as if their day had really arrived only to note that interest seemed to fade away again just as quickly.

In theory there seems to be few activities for which they could not be used and many ambitious hopes were raised only to find that the hardware proved rather more intractable than had been supposed.

Interest began to be aroused once more as more capable electronic systems were developed along with greater reliability, less weight and perhaps, more importantly, lower power demands.

Electronic companies and manufacturers of small engines were aware of the possibilities but there seemed to be several false dawns along the way. In 1962 the US Navy deployed a Ryan Firebee over Cuba following the loss of a U-2, and during the Vietnam War more than 3000 RPV missions were mounted over the North of the country.

Right: The Israeli-built Scout which has proved so successful in the recent Lebanese War.

Below: The experimental LRV-2 remotely piloted microlite developed by NASA's Dryden Flight Research Facility.

The Machan research RPV which is fitted with a digital flight control system and is operated via a data link from a ground control station.

Right: The Aquila demonstrates its take-off and retrieval techniques.

Despite the high hopes it seemed that the RPV was in limbo and a somewhat exasperated US General Accounting Office suggested that the only real barrier to the development of battlefield RPVs was "user apathy" – in other words, a marked reluctance to replace a manned aircraft with an unmanned vehicle. This rather tetchy remark was no doubt prompted by some of the inter-service politics that tends to cloud so many issues in the West though it was not the whole reason. To someone on the sideline it seemed that the trouble actually lay with the protagonists of RPVs themselves.

Was the delay due simply to the fact that it could not be decided if military use of these machines was to emphasise expendable or returnable systems? The idea of cheap expendables is attractive, while the concept of a more complex system which could be used many times over also has its merits. Perhaps the real answer to that must lie in the choice of payload.

There is no doubt that the RPVs offer several useful roles at a relatively inexpensive cost. They can perform surveillance, reconnaissance and electronic warfare missions, and in naval use would suggest a useful application in over-the-horizon targeting.

A considerable amount of basic work was being conducted in Europe and the United States, and allowing for the difficulty of recovering the RPV at sea the naval role appeared to be the most popular at one time. Their use in this role envisaged mission equipment to include several sensors, a navigation package and a data link system. It was recognised that the requirement for shipborne compatibility was even more demanding from an engineering viewpoint. The RPV had to be small with high standards of reliability and maintainability, while electromagnetic compatibility, as well as

with other ship's systems, was of prime importance. These factors inevitably dictated a fairly complex weapon system in a small package and caused a degree of "backing off" by the intended users.

Manufacturers continued to work and develop systems and a large number of drones and targets had been produced in many parts of the world. In the United States the Compass Cope high altitude, long endurance RPV programme was extremely ambitious and was proving successful when terminated in 1977.

It would seem the catalyst for a change of mind came with the realisation that the Israeli's were using RPVs in the Bekaa Valley and the extremely good results that were being obtained.

Perhaps it is entirely coincidental that at the same time budgetary pressures were making it increasingly necessary to look at lower cost applications, many of which were eminently suitable for RPV applications. Meanwhile mounting evidence of Israeli success with RPVs was forcing greater attention as conclusive proof was gained that in certain applications RPVs are a practical, economic alternative to conventional manned aircraft. In simple terms they not only save money, they save lives.

It was soon apparent that Israeli spokesmen were much in demand at various conferences and seminars with many nations anxious to gain first hand knowledge. Interest had been stimulated in all parts of the

A Tucan prepared for launch. It can operate over a distance of 70 km (43.5 miles) and transmits video data to the ground station.

world, with Sweden going on record that it would require an operational RPV within five years.

At one such presentation details of the use of the Israeli Scout were given and suggested an organisational frame and force structure. Fitted with a TV camera and an aerial photographic camera the Scout can be used for real time reconnaissance and surveillance, battlefield observation, artillery targeting, directing close air support strikes and for anti-smuggling border patrols.

The Scout system comprises an independent flight section while sections can be grouped in platoons or companies. This approach is said to simplify logistics and improve force allocation. Alternatively the section can be attached to a division or corps. This approach

can provide better support for the corps commander, according to his needs.

The smallest Scout section comprises just 12 men and four trucks and several aircraft. A typical deployment is to have two or three aircraft on a mission, one aircraft on launcher as a stand-by and the other aircraft on reserve or maintenance.

The system is highly mobile, all units having been designed for ease of fitment on standard army trucks. On reaching the required site the maintenance crew prepare the first aircraft and the control station crew prepare the ground control element. The complete section can be ready for action within an hour.

The extensive experience of RPV operation gained by Israel in the recent war in Lebanon is now being used to develop a new generation of aircraft. It is understood that a greater degree of automation is being sought to reduce dependence upon ground control and

Above: The Locust, a new design shown at the Paris Air Show 1983. (A. T. Hogg)

Below: Like a moth impaled in a museum, the Aquila RPV on show at Farnborough, 1982. (A. T. Hogg)

improved navigation sensors have been developed. Expense will be reduced by the use of microprocessor components in place of some of the current navigation devices and it is possible that an element of satellite navigation will be introduced.

Recently it was reported in the international press that a South African built version of the Scout had been shot down over Mozambique. Details of alleged payload are sparse, though it is claimed that it was carrying a camera of French origin.

Another basic decision regarding RPVs is whether to make a fixed-wing or rotary-wing aircraft. Each has its own peculiar advantages, and in the case of rotary-wing aircraft they can be used in forest clearings and other areas of inhospitable topography. They do tend to present problems of control, and payloads are not as good as those obtained with fixed-wing designs.

Although there have been a considerable number of drone programmes in the United States, and an even greater number of RPV projects that have foundered, there is now just one battlefield RPV in being. This is the Aquila, of which the US Army is expected to receive more than 700. Implementation was originally scheduled for 1985 but budget cuts appeared to have caused this date to slip back to the financial year 1988. Another international collaborative programme – Locust – has been terminated which seems to suggest the old routine all over again.

This leaves Aquila as the only active RPV development programme in the US and its initial payload will be a daylight TV camera only. Development of a day/night forward-looking infra-red device is under way but is not expected to be used for operational purposes before the end of the decade.

The Aquila launch system comprises a vehicle-mounted hydraulic catapult and recovery is by a vertical, truck mounted net. Recovery is automatic by day or night and is achieved by a nose-mounted infra-red

Above: The newest Canadair design, the CL-227, relies upon helicopter technology. (A. T. Hogg)

Left: The Canadiar CL-89 was one of the first service RPVs to abandon the appearance of an aircraft. (I. V. Hogg)

beacon which is detected by two IR cameras mounted on the net structure. Approach path errors are detected by these cameras and this information is transmitted to the RPV via a data link. A back-up system uses the payload sensor for guidance. If both of these devices fail the aircraft can be recovered by a parachute system.

Aquila has considerable potential for development and can be used as a platform for just about all the usual roles including one that is probably not quite so usual – psychological warfare. This is expected to include the dropping of leaflets, and loudspeaker broadcasts using a voice playback system. These are considered to be deep penetration missions based upon extended dead reckoning modes to allow it to fly beyond the range of the normal data link control.

It is obvious of course that Aquila stands for the expensive end of the RPV range and many countries would be happy with less sophisticated systems that would be more than adequate for the mundane tasks.

This represents the simpler approach which is close to the expendable philosophy.

Work in Germany has resulted in a number of aircraft including the Mini-Drone and the Toucan which is serving as the basis for more advanced RPVs for use against ground targets. The Toucan programme is benefiting from some of the expertise gained in the now defunct Locust programme so perhaps all is not lost in that quarter. A feature of the new RPV family will be the ability to seek out and attack targets independently.

British firms have also produced an interesting line of drones, aerial targets and RPVs. More recently a new version of Stabileye has been flown and the Machan has joined in as a demonstrator vehicle for a variety of payloads. Sky Eye is another using a basic radio control system. Stability is induced by a system of wingtip sensors which measure the earth's electrostatic field and allows a precise measurement of height to be derived. The on-board controller then ensures that the

The Snipe, a design of RPV with the virtues of cheapness and simplicity. Notice the open parachute assembly and the sensor unit mounted under the wing. (I. V. Hogg)

measurement at each sensor is matched as closely as possible thus keeping the wingtips at equal distance from the ground and creating the desired stability.

Much of this interest in the UK has been concerned with the Phoenix proposal for a battlefield RPV to meet British Army requirements. This programme has already been the subject of much research, and in May 1983 the UK Ministry of Defence ordered eight Stabileyes in addition to an earlier ten for a flight research programme using MOD developed ground stations and payloads.

By the beginning of 1983 the Phoenix programme had firmed up on a fixed wing configuration with two teams of electronic/airframe manufacturers in final contention. By April these teams had been awarded an engineering study contract. The Phoenix system is intended to perform remote targeting and surveillance by day or night and will comprise three main elements. These are the air vehicle, a mobile ground control station and a remotely deployed ground data terminal. The RPV will be capable of operating either autonomously, using its own on-board flight guidance system, or under remote control from the ground via a two way radio link. This multi-channel microwave link will provide secure transmission of data including real-time

video. Digital spread spectrum modulation techniques provide high security, low detectability and a degree of immunity to deliberate jamming. It is a flexible device with multiple frequency band options providing optimum choice of frequency for any particular applications.

The most recent British RPV is the Hawkeye intended as a rugged, simple RPV designed to operate at brigade or equivalent level, with a fast response and turn-round time and requiring only minimal ground support. It has been designed with the express purpose of providing the maximum number of customer options from close range still photography through to deep penetration missions carrying a real-time TV payload.

Certainly there now seems to be a new attitude towards RPV systems and several rather unorthodox systems have inevitably surfaced in this new search for originality and adaptability. Microlight aircraft suggest a useful role and the ability to revert quickly to normal manned operation.

In a series of trials in the United States under NASA supervision an RPV microlight under the designation LRV-2 (Low Reynolds Vehicle No 2) was fitted with a lightweight autopilot, a radio control uplink, a nose-mounted TV, a radar transponder for precise tracking and a telemetry system for research data.

The lightweight autopilot is an experimental system that is gyroless and has no moving parts though precise

The Westland Wisp, an experimental RPV using helicopter
technology. (Westland Helicopters Ltd)

An AEL project seen at Farnborough, and advertised as being suitable for both military and commercial applications. (A. T. Hogg)

details are not known. It is suggested that future high altitude solar-powered aircraft may use similar systems. The control surfaces all have a large projection forward of the hingeline to minimise hinge moments and so reduce the loading on the small electric actuators. The initial tests were largely aerodynamic in nature and featured flights up to 6100 m (20 000 ft) in altitude.

France has provided a distinctly Gallic flavour to RPVs with a remotely piloted airship for both civil and military roles. Known as Dino 3 the airship has a volume of 95 m³ (3355 ft³) and can carry a payload of around 10 kg (4.5 lb). It is controlled via a seven channel radio link similar to that used by model aircraft constructors. It has been suggested that Dino could be used for surveillance, submarine detection and aerial photography.

It is interesting to note that one of the latest American ideas is for an expendable mini drone for the US Air Force. A development contract has been awarded for 14 YCGM-121A Pave Tiger vehicles. The aircraft is intended to carry a wide range of payloads and will fly a pre-programmed mission. On-board sensors will provide data to the microprocessor-controlled navigation system.

Pave Tiger will be used to aid tactical aircraft and the key to the success of this project will be low cost.

It would seem that there is to be a place for the sophisticated and the lowly expendable in the future electronic battlefield. What is less evident is the fact that the military forces are still not quite sure what to do about RPVs. One thing at least is certain, RPVs are cost effective solutions to many battlefield problems. When this is accepted the other certainty that is now emerging is that the equipment needs to be simple, easily transportable, reliable and feature a fair amount of automation.

One Hundred Years Ago

Ian V. Hogg

Maxim's original machine gun; the mechanism had several differences to that eventually adopted and the whole weapon was cumbersome.

1883 and 1884 were harrowing years for the British as they watched a succession of near-disasters unfold in the Sudan, an area which had come under British control unbidden as a result of the conquest of Egypt. The Sudan of the period has been described as "a million square miles of desert, swamp, rock, thorn and scrub where, under its blistering, baking sun, lived a medley of savage and uncongenial tribes." Its only home industry appeared to be slave-trading, which the British were anxious to suppress, but the immense distances and paucity of communications meant that very little impression was actually made on the country.

During the battles in Egypt, by which Sir Garnet Wolseley defeated Ahmed Arabi and his armies, a religious leader arose in the Sudan, calling himself "El Mahdi," the Messiah. He rapidly assembled an army

One of the first service Maxim guns was this British .45-in model with brass water jacket. It is shown here mounted on the "Overbank" carriage, for firing from behind parapets.

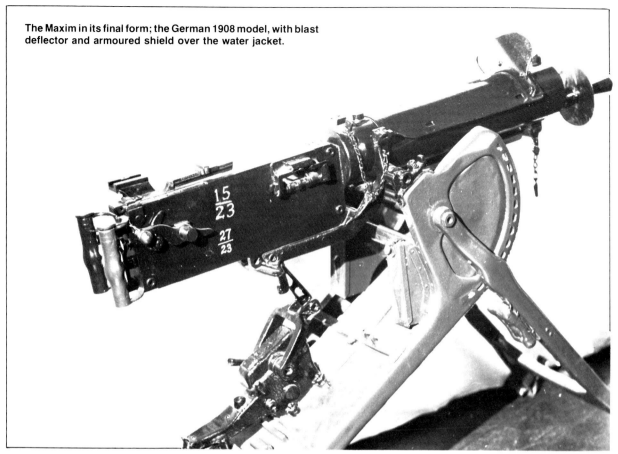

The Maxim in its final form; the German 1908 model, with blast deflector and armoured shield over the water jacket.

from the tribesmen and roughly handled several detachments of Egyptian troops sent to deal with him. Each victory attracted more followers, and soon El Mahdi controlled most of the Sudan.

Britain had every intention of withdrawing her army from Egypt as soon as possible and tried to avoid entanglements in the Sudan, but since the Egyptians could not make any impression on the Mahdi, the usual political compromise was reached; the British Army would have nothing to do with the matter, but a Colonel Hicks, on the point of retiring, was appointed to command the Egyptian Army in the Sudan. He was given a few British officers to assist him, whereupon honour was satisfied and the British government washed its hands of the problem.

Hicks Pasha, as he came to be called, since he was now a General, had an average military career behind him; commissioned into the Bombay Army in 1840 he had served in the Indian Mutiny and one or two minor campaigns thereafter and had spent almost his entire life in India. With his force of Egyptian troops he set out in search of the Mahdi and, meeting a small force at Jebel 'Ayn, south of Khartoum in April 1883, defeated them soundly. This did his morale a great deal of good, and, expanding his force to about 10 000 he set off again, this time to find the Mahdi's main army and defeat it.

After several weeks of hot and dry marching, the two armies met at Kashgil, on 5 November 1883. Unfortunately the meeting was not as planned by Hicks Pasha; the Mahdi's force lay in ambush, fell on Hicks' army and cut it to pieces. Not one man appears to have survived.

There now appeared another ex-British officer, Val-

The Greek 1903 Mannlicher rifle, the only service rifle to use the rotating Schoenauer magazine.

entine Baker. He had a varied career, starting as a farmer, becoming a soldier, fighting in the Kaffir War and the Crimean War, and then suddenly being dismissed the service for indecently assaulting a young lady in a railway carriage. After serving a year in prison, Baker went East and immediately became a major-general in the Turkish Army. When the British began rebuilding the Egyptian Army, after Wolseley's campaigns, their first thought was to offer Baker the command, but their second thought was that the other officers might not take kindly to being commanded by a man cashiered for indecent assault. They therefore offered Baker command of the Gendarmerie, a para-military police-cum-internal security force. Considering that this was probably as good a way to see action as any, and perhaps a good way or reinstating himself, Baker accepted.

Six weeks after the massacre at Kashgil, Baker and a small force of Gendarmerie landed at Suakin, on the Red Sea, with orders to protect the port, which was the Sudan's only seaport, and prevent it falling to the Mahdi's supporters. He had been given strict orders not to risk his small force by taking the initiative; merely sit tight and look after Suakin.

As might have been foreseen, he didn't obey; after a few weeks of chafing, he mustered what force he could and set forth in search of Osman Digna, the Mahdi's local commander. Marching with 3500 men, Baker scattered a few parties of Dervishes (the name now given to the Mahdi's followers by the British) and, like Hicks, blundered straight into a massive ambush at El Teb. The Egyptian soldiery, terrified of the Dervishes, fled, the Sudanese followed suit, and the Europeans were cut to pieces. In all 96 officers and 2225 men were slaughtered, though Baker managed to escape.

This defeat was soon followed by the fall of another town in the neighbourhood to Osman Digna, and now, at last, the British in Egypt finally sent a force of British troops to try and salvage something from the wreckage. In February 1884 3000 regular army troops and a naval detachment landed at Trinkitat, on the Red Sea. They were commanded by LtGen Gerald Graham VC, with Redvers Buller as his second-in-command, and Graham's orders were to advance to Tokar and relieve the Egyptian garrison there, under siege from Osman Digna. By the time the force landed, Tokar had fallen,

Watching for the Dervishes: a contemporary drawing showing an officer and his staff outside a square, waiting for the enemy to attack.

Above: The Naval Brigade at El Teb, firing Gatling and Nordenfelt machine guns. A sketch made on the spot, though the artist names the Nordenfelt guns as Gardners.

Below: Hicks Pasha (seated, second from right) with his staff.

Some of El Mahdi's troops with a gun captured from Hicks Pasha's forces.

but Graham, "not exactly brilliant" according to Wolseley, nevertheless followed his orders and marched on the town. As he passed El Teb, the scene of Baker's defeat, 6000 Dervishes were waiting and, without further ado, charged.

The British troops formed square and, by superior firepower, managed to beat off the attack for no more than 189 casualties, one of whom was Valentine Baker, wounded in the face. Graham resumed his march to Tokar, found nothing to do there, so turned about and marched back to Trinkitat. There was nothing to do there, either, so after a few weeks rest he set out again, this time to find Osman Digna's main army and defeat it. On 11 March 1884 he arrived at Tamai and, once more, several thousand Dervishes descended on his force. And it was here that the impossible took place; the Dervishes broke the British square, an incident immortalised by Kipling. The guns of the Naval Brigade were captured, but the square was rapidly reformed, the Dervishes evicted, the guns retaken, and eventually the Dervishes (the "Fuzzy-Wuzzies" as the British troops nicknamed them, from their hair-style) were defeated. Whether it was the York & Lancaster Regiment or the Black Watch who had given way is something never satisfactorily resolved, but certainly the Black Watch took it most to heart; for many years afterwards the private soldiers of other regiments, looking for some innocent diversion, would simply call out "Broken Square!" in the hearing of the Black Watch, and a satisfactory brawl would always ensue.

Graham's force, having demonstrated that the Dervishes were not invincible, was soon withdrawn, and Osman Digna regained control of the area. But all this was but the opening shots of the campaign which was to finish with General Gordon in Khartoum in the following year, and to which we will return in due course.

The other major military milestone of 1883–84 was taking place far from the Sudan, in a small workshop at 57D Hatton Garden, London. Here Hiram Stevens Maxim was hard at work examining ways of making a firearm into an automatic weapon.

Maxim was born in Sangersville, Maine, in 1840, and in spite of very little formal education he soon displayed an aptitude for mechanical engineering. Apprenticed first to a carriage maker, he went on to make agricultural implements and then set up and operated his own mill. After other pastimes, including being the bouncer in a bar (for he was a powerful young man) he worked with his uncle in the manufacture of gas lighting equipment. Maxim invented an improved model, which his uncle began making, then made an even better design; this infuriated his uncle, who had just finished tooling-up for the first model, and he fired Maxim. He moved to Boston and invented a sprinkler fire extinguisher for warehouses which is the ancestor of all the automatic systems used today, and then he went into the new science of electricity, inventing an electric light bulb. As a result of this he travelled to

Dover Turret, on the Admiralty Pier. The introduction of the 16-in (406 mm) muzzle-loaders, which are still inside the turret, was mentioned in last year's edition; 1983 celebrates the centenary of the first firing of the guns, on 16 July 1883. The door at lower right leads to the engine rooms and magazines, buried in the depths of the pier.

Paris in 1881 to see the International Electrical Exhibition.

There, as he later recounted, he met a friend of his, "An Austrian Jew, who said to me 'Hang your electricity! If you want to make your fortune, invent something which will allow these foolish Europeans to cut each other's throats with greater facility!' " Maxim took his advice, retired from the electrical business, set up his workshop in Hatton Garden, and began investigating what made guns work and how they might be made to work automatically. Between 1883 and 1885 he examined every possible method, patented all those which appeared to have promise, and settled down to develop a gun working by utilising the force of recoil. He completed his first model in 1884 and demonstrated it to the Duke of Cambridge, Lord Wolseley and a number of staff officers. Although it worked, it was somewhat cumbersome and, acting on the suggestions of some of Wolseley's staff, he made modifications and refined the design into its final form. The rest is history. His original gun was later presented to the Science Museum, South Kensington, but by some unrecorded means left there and is now in the Museum of the US Marine Corps at Quantico.

1 April 1884 saw the granting of British Patent 5793/1884 to G. E. Vaughan, for a "bolt-action rifle magazine." Vaughan was, in fact, a Patent Agent, and the inventor of the device was Otto Schoenauer,

manager of the Österreichische Waffenfabriks-gesellschaft of Steyr. The patent covered a unique revolving magazine which could be charger-loaded through the open bolt of the rifle and which then fed the rounds by spring action, revolving a spool which held the cartridges so as to present a fresh cartridge into the boltway whenever the bolt was opened. At that time Schoenauer's company was busy manufacturing rifles to the designs of von Mannlicher, and two rifles with the spool magazine appeared in the 1880s. It was not until 1903, however, that the idea was accepted for military use, in the Greek service 6.5 mm Mannlicher-Schoenauer rifle of that year.

In spite of its apparently poor reception by military purchasers, the rotary magazine was soon adopted by commercial users and appeared in a wide range of Mannlicher sporting rifles and carbines from the 1890s onward. It earns its place here by virtue of the fact that it is still in military service; the contemporary Steyr SSG Sniping Rifle uses an up-to-date version of the magazine which Schoenauer patented one hundred years ago.